DEATH LOG

Compiled by James Romenesko

Police Beat Press 2101 W. Wisconsin Ave. Milwaukee, WI 53233

Library of Congress Catalog Card No.: 82-90083

ISBN 0-942724-00-3

Police Beat Press
James Romenesko, Editor
2101 W. Wisconsin Ave.
Milwaukee, WI 53233

Manufactured in the United States of America
First Printing February 1982
10 9 8 7 6 5 4 3 2 1

Acknowledgements

Special thanks go to the employes of the Milwaukee County Medical Examiner's Office, to Ed at the On Broadway Plays store, to Jim and Tom at Econo-Print, to Bob Greene of the Chicago Tribune, and to friends who believed in this book. And finally, thanks to my parents, Merlin and Rosemary, and to my brothers and sisters for their support.

"It is the denial of death that is partially responsible for people living empty, purposeless lives; for when you live as if you'll live forever, it becomes too easy to postpone the things you know that you must do."

- Elisabeth Kubler-Ross
from *Death - the Final Stage of Growth*

Death Log

Introduction

I don't like the sight of blood. In fact, I hate it. Several years ago, I nearly fainted after seeing blood spurt from the backside of a bull at a bullfight in Mexico. So, you can imagine how I felt reading my first coroner's report, which was a grisly tale of a young man who stuck his head out of a freight elevator at the wrong time. It was a detailed account that left little to the imagination. Every wound and every dismembered limb was documented in the report. About midway through the case, I decided I had had enough and stopped reading.

However, I didn't bat an eye two weeks later as I read a report on a vicious double homicide. In the heat of deadline, I guess, you do what you have to do. And this time, I was prepared to read the worst. Now that I think back, the elevator case was tame compared to some other reports I have read at the Milwaukee County Medical Examiner's Office, which I am assigned to cover for The Milwaukee Journal.

Morgue reports are fascinating studies of human behavior. They are often bizarre, depressing and incredibly tragic. The "best" of them — the most unusual ones — are shared over drinks by cops, coroners and reporters who cover the morgue. The cases in DEATH LOG are the most unusual I have come across in the past five years as a police reporter. Many of the cases in this book were never reported in newspapers. They were simply too gruesome or exposed bizarre sexual indiscretions on the part of the deceased — indiscretions that shouldn't be described in family newspapers.

The first version of DEATH LOG was printed in March of 1981, with an investment of $35. It was a slim 48 pages, printed at my neighborhood economy quick-print shop, and sold in only one Milwaukee store. Sales were sluggish until a Milwaukee newspaper — not my own — wrote about the book. Then, within hours, my first printing of fewer than 50 books sold out. Other newspaper articles about DEATH LOG spurred mail orders from around the country. Detecting great reader interest in morgue reports, I wrote to several publishers and tried to have the book printed in an expanded form for national distribution. The message from each publisher was the same: DEATH LOG is too gruesome for us. I then decided to form my own publishing company, Police Beat Press, to print and distribute the book.

The Milwaukee County reports appear as they were written by the investigators. Only names, addresses, telephone numbers and other identifying factors have been blacked out to avoid unnecessary grief or embarrassment for survivors. Some of the older reports from Los Angeles County are difficult to read because of poor reproduction and sloppy handwriting. The handwritten reports are included in the book, but are followed by a newly typed account for easier reading.

James Romenesko
Milwaukee, Wisconsin

Menagerie of animals, some frozen, found in dead man's home

MILWAUKEE COUNTY MEDICAL EXAMINER

CASE NO. 1615

SUPPLEMENTARY

Name GEORGE W. ████
Date Death 9/1/80

Monday, 9/1/80, 5:40PM, Capt Thelen of the Milwaukee Detective Bureau called to report that squad 106 is standing by at 1655 South 16th Street. An 82 year old gentleman by name of GEORGE W. ████, dob 5-15-1898, was found in a cool and rigid state. Medical Examiner requested. No relatives are at scene.

5:50PM, Met at ████ South 16th Street, an old frame single dwelling by POs Jack Deering and Robert Farkas of squad 60 and Detective Apps of 106. In the kitchen draped over a table chair is the cool and rigid body of GEORGE W. ████. The deceased had apparently been in a seated position facing the table towards the west and then collapsed to his right. His left hand is resting on the table with his head in a down position to the north beneath the level of the chair seat. The entire residence is very cluttered and contains numerous bird cages with birds. Weasel or mink type animals are caged in the basement. There are numerous caged birds on the second floor as well. Also on the second floor in the closet is a family of mice who acted as being a part of the household. Three cats and one dog have been removed by the Humane Society. There is bird and animal food and droppings about the entire residence. There is currency and much coin in evidence in the living room. There are capped vials of medication in the refrigerator as well as on a living room table. There are three frozen birds in the freezer together with frozen food. A friend of the deceased, Emma ████ 73, dob 5-6-1907, of ████ West Wisconsin Avenue 342-████, was present. Ms. ████ said that she has known the deceased since 1926. He never married and he has no family and no known relatives. She said the deceased was on Social Security and also received a company pension, name of his company not known to the informant. The deceased was being treated by Dr. Mayer for his heart, stomach, and arthritis. He also had a hernia. Ms. ████ said that she last saw the deceased this past Friday at 9am when she picked up his bills and money to pay them for him. He was in good spirits and was hopping around on one foot due to his hernia condition. She called him today beginning with this morning. Not getting any response, she notified the police who accompanied her to the residence. The front door of the residence, actually side door, was secured. They went around to the rear and entered from the cellar door which was closed but unlocked. However, there did not appear to be anything suspicious about the premises nor did the cluttered state suggest that any struggle had taken place. Ms. ████ said that the deceased had mentioned a couple of weeks ago that a girl by the name of Lorna had "frenched" him on the 4th of July. By this she meant that Lorna had either played, bitten, or who knows what with his private parts. ████ also said that the deceased had known Lorna for about 4 or 5 years and that she had worked about four years ago at the Forest Home Cemetery. The deceased had mentioned to ████ that Lorna was after his money. ████ did not know Lorna's last name or where she lived. There were numerous large photos of a male dressed in various women's clothing. Whether these were of the deceased during an earlier time is a question. Ms. ████ said, however, that the deceased had taken pictures about the residence although she would not admit to these pictures being of the deceased. Ms. ████ insisted that the deceased was to go to the Voth and Anderson Funeral Home and that she was to take care of the burial arrangements. They were called and removed the body to the Medical Examiner's office. All animals and birds were removed to either the Humane Society or the Police District 6. The currency and coin together with the medication were removed to the Medical Examiner's office by the undersigned in the company of PO Jack Deering with a signed property receipt obtained. The residence was securred by the police department. Checked with neighbors Arlene ████ and Roman ████ of ████ South 16th Street. They said that they have been living here for the past 25 yearsand have known the deceased all during this period. They used to see him

OVER

outside almost every day until the past couple of weeks. He has since had what they thought may have been the flu and he seemed to have a lot of congestion. They have not seen him for a couple of weeks. They know of no relatives.

C. Borchardt

Tuesday September 2,1980 Note: Investigator Thomas F. Hanratty had received a call from Rachel [redacted] of the City Desk at the Milwaukee Sentinael. Informant stated that she had received a call from one LORNA [redacted] of Wautoma,Wisconsin - phone 1-787[redacted]. It was learned that LORNA [redacted] is a good friend of the deceased GEORGE [redacted]. She planned to contact a funeral home.

David W. Livingston

9/2/80 8:50 AM ETHEL [redacted], 166 N. [redacted] St., 258[redacted], called this office and states that she saw an article in the Milwaukee Sentinal this morning about the death of GEORGE W. [redacted]. She states that her mother, MRS. ALTA [redacted], [redacted] A S. 17th St., 672[redacted], is a first cousin to the deceased. She states that she believes that there are other cousins. She states that she has not, as yet, notified her mother of the death. She states that after she has done this she will contact this office relative to funeral arrangements.

Robert E. Schultz

9/2/80 11:10 AM ETHEL [redacted], above, called this office and stated that family members were contacting the deceased's attorney, MR. TALSKY, this afternoon. She states that it is all right with the family if funeral arrangements are continued by the Voth - Anderson Funeral Home.

Robert E. Schultz

Tuesday September 2,80 12:20PM The undersigned spoke with Dr. H. Meyer regarding his treatment of George [redacted], age 82. The doctor stated that he has been treating the subject for years because of ASHD and Hypertension. The doctor last spoke with the subject in May of this year therefore the doctor wishes this office issue the death certificate.

R. Goeb

Baby mauled to death by pet dog

MILWAUKEE COUNTY MEDICAL EXAMINER

CASE NO. 333

SUPPLEMENTARY

Name James Glenn ████████

Date Death 2-11-80

Monday, February 11, 1980: 2:40AM: Received a call from Lt. HOLUBOWICZ, District # 6, requesting an investigator at 2010 West ██████. Informant stated that the body of James Glenn ████████, age, 3 1/2 weeks, date of birth, 1-15-80 was at the above location and had allegedly been malled by a dog.

E. Himmelreich (wlh) EH

2-11-80: 2:45AM: Investigator E. Himmelreich dispatched to the scene.

E. Himmelreich (wlh) EH

2/11/80,3:00 AM.

Met with Dets., Dobesh and Coulter #106 and PO.Kellam and Lazewski #34 at 2010 West ████████ Street, and older South side flat. The residence appears neat and clean. There are three bedrooms, all on the east side of the residence, one off the living room, one off the dining room and one off the kitchen. The residence is that of the maternal grandmother, Evelyn M. ████████, age 56, dob-7/27/1923, (643█████). The deceased's mother Bernadette S.████████ age 17, dob-7/24/1962, single, lived at 2834 South ████ Street, (643█████). The mother has not been feeling well, since the birth of the deceased. The deceased has been staying with the grandmother since this past Friday,2/8/80.

Cursory examination of the deceased, who was lying on the kitchen table, discloses a male infant identified as JAMES GLENN ████████, 28 days old, dob-1/15/1980. The head is severely lacerated, the left eye appears collapsed, and there are numerous circular teeth marks and eccymosis to the legs and upper chest and back. The body is cool and limp.

The deceased slept on a single bed in the bedroom off the dining room. Inspection of this bedroom discloses some blood spots on the rug.

According to the grandmother, Evelyn, the deceased was born prematurly, was kept at the hospital, Trinity, for about two weeks before being released. The deceased's mother has been having hemorrhaging problems since coming home from the hospital. The doctor advised the mother to take it easy for a few days and get off her feet, to probably correct this difficulty. Therefore the deceased was brought to the grandmothers residence, this past Friday, where the grandmother and some of her other daughters, who live there, could help take care of the deceased.

The grandmother has had a Siberian Husky dog for the past 7½ years She got it as a pup. The dog has run of the house, has never attacked nor biten any one. The dog has never made any attempt to bite the dece or made any type of action toward the deceased. He would sit up and sniff the deceased while it was being fed. The dog was fed earlier this evening and there were dishes of food in the kitchen at this time, which the husky and another dog,(a puppy of mixed parentage) can eat out of any time.

The deceased, after being fed at about 12:15 AM, was put to bed in the middle bedroom. The grandmother checked the deceased at about 12:45 AM, then went to bed in the front bedroom. The Husky sleeps under the grandmother's bed. Around 2:00 AM, the grandmother awakened knowing that the deceased should be fed, but she didn't hear it crying. It did cry rather softly. She went to check, saw the deceased was not in bed, saw the blood spots on the bedroom rug. The only thin she could think of,was the dog. She went looking for the dog, and fou him in his usual place under her bed, the deceased was lying face down next to the dog. The grandmother called her son-in-law, Bob ███████, of 3348 South ██████, who called the police. The grandmother picked up the deceased and put him on the kitchen table. The grandmother did not hear any unusual sounds during the night.

2/11/80, 3:55 AM

Dets. Dobesh and Coulter made notification of the deceased's death to the mother.

The police have taken the Husky to the Humane Society.

E.Himmelreich EH

Monday February 11,1980; 1:14PM

Drove to 2010 West ████ Street with Detectives R. KRUSICK and G. MITCHELL, along with Lt. Newmann. Interviewed one GARY CHRISTOPHOR ████, 25 years old, DOB 4/12/1954, the uncle of the deceased JAMES ████. The informant works at Evinrude Motors full time and part time as a mechanic at Marshall Motors. Because he had worked both jobs for the past couple of days, and had been awake for the past 20 hours, he slept through the commotion surrounding the finding of the deceased's body. The informant laid down of the couch at about 10:30PM after arriving at the home. The dog Inooki was under the bed of the grandmother when the informant went to bed. The dog, while frequently taking bones , shoes, boots and toys under the bed, had not played with a stuffed toy, as far as the informant knows. No bruising was noticed on the baby at any time.

Drove to the residence of another relative and met with the grandmother EVELYN ████. She stated that she gave the baby a bath on Sunday morning at about 9:00AM and there were no bruises on the baby at that time. The child was changed by various aunts of the baby during the day an no brusing was seen. The child was placed face up on the bed in a middle bedroom, put in a drawer-bed, surrounded by pillows and a stuffed toy teddy bear placed on the bed next to him. Several times, the grandmother went into the room and checked on the child and gave the baby his pacifier. At about 12:30AM, the child was checked and was sleeping so the grandmother went to bed. About one-half hour later, the grandmother put the child's bottle on the stove and entered the child's bedroom. The baby was gone and the teddy bear was on the floor next to the bed. The child's clothing was missing with the child, except for a blanket on the bed. Blood spots were seen on the floor next to the bed and on the bed covering itself. The grandmother searched for the child and went into her own bedroom, looked under the bed and found the child lying between the paws of the dog.

Spoke to BERNADETTE ████, the mother of the child, and she gave essentially the same story as before. The child was brought to the grandmother's home on Friday. A quiet child, the baby did not squirm about or cry, and was too small to turn over by itself. A sister , KATHRYN ████, 22 years old, who stays with the grandmother, stated that the baby was somewhat ill with colic on Sunday, but the grandmother denies this. The sister said that the child would sometimes spit up milk and had done so on Sunday. Kathryn was asleep at the time of the incident.

2/11/80; 3:30PM

Drove to the Wisconsin Humane Society with Dr. Samuels and she examined the dog Inooki, Dr. Samuels compared the teeth and paw marks with those found on the deceased JAMES ████.

Thomas F. Hanratty

Man awakened by wife; slays her

MILWAUKEE COUNTY MEDICAL EXAMINER

CASE NO. ...723......

SUPPLEMENTARY

Name Chun Sun [redacted]
Date Death April 7,81

Tuesday April 7,81 3:55PM Capt. Pape, District #2 called this office and stated that the body of Chun Sun [redacted], DOB 5/1/40 has been found at [redacted] S. 13 St. The officer requested an investigator be dispatched to the scene.

R. Goeb *RG*

TUESDAY, APRIL 7, 1981, 4:25 P.M.
The undersigned arrived at the residence of CHUN SON [redacted], Korean female, 40 years old, date of birth 5-1-1940, residence: [redacted] South 13 Street, phone 281[redacted], who is married to OSCAR [redacted] of the same address.

Upon arrival, the undersigned was met by Lieutenant Brandt, Detectives Repischek and Jankowski. Also on the scene was Police Officer Schoenecker, Squad 296, who took 50 photos at the scene; all officers are from the Milwaukee Police Department.

Police Officer Olsen, Squad 64, was the first officer on the scene. He stated that he arrived at 3:30 P.M. this date and was admitted into the residence by OSCAR [redacted] at 3:33 P.M. Police Officer Olsen asked Mr. [redacted]: "Did you shoot your wife?"; Mr. [redacted] replied "Yes!" Officer Olsen then asked Mr. [redacted]: "Is she dead?"; Mr. [redacted] replied "Yes!"

The undersigned was directed to the bedroom on the first floor of the 2 family dwelling. There the body of the deceased was seen lying face up with the head against the east wall, and the feet pointing southwest. Multiple small bone fragments are lying near the legs of the deceased and 2 bone fragments were lying on a chair located in the corner where the east and south walls meet. A missile fragment was lying on the floor 6 inches from the waist of the deceased's right side.

There were 4 bullet holes noted in the bedroom:

1. One was located on the south wall 3 feet and 7 inches from the floor and 6-1/2 inches from the frame of the door.

2. One was located on the south wall 6 feet and 1-1/2 inches from the floor and 10 inches from the frame of the door.

3. The third was located in the ceiling 3 feet and 3 inches from the south wall and 2 feet and 4 inches from the east wall.

4. The fourth was also located in the ceiling 3 feet and 3/4 inch from the east wall and 3 feet and 1 inch from the north wall.

Small amounts of hair, blood, and brain material were seen on the south wall and southeast corner of the ceiling.

A cursory examination of the body revealed it to be that of an Oriental female dreseed in indoor clothing, except for shoes or socks. An entrance wound could be seen in the right temporal area. An exit wound could be seen in the left temporo-parietal area. Copious amounts of liquid and clotted blood were found under the head of the deceased.

According to police informants, the weapon used was a .357, 6-shot, Magnum handgun which was lying on the dresser, which is located on the north wall. Examination of the gun revealed no live rounds. On the gun was the following information: Hawes Fire Arms Company, J. P. Sauer & Sohn, No. 49135. The above-described handgun was removed from the residence by the police officers and is now on their inventory.

Police informants stated that the upstairs neighbor, EDWARD S. , date of birth 6-7-1927, phone 282 , who resides in the upper flat, same address as that of the deceased, stated that he heard 4 or 5 noises around 3:00 P.M. this date.

The undersigned interviewed MICHAEL W. , date of birth 5-6-1948, residence: West Edgerton Avenue, phone 529- , who is the Operation Manager at Trans Con Lines, 5300 South 13 Street, phone 282- . Informant stated that Mr. called him between 3:15 and 3:20 P.M. this date and stated "Take me off the board. I just shot my wife." and without further comment, Mr. hung up. Informant stated that Mr. came to the office this date about 9:30 A.M. to check if there was any work for him. He was informed that there may be work available later in the day. Informant stated that Mr. is a truck driver for Trans Con Lines.

Police informants stated that Mr. called the police after shooting his wife. Informants stated that the reason given by Mr. was that he was upset because his wife woke him up.

The hands of the deceased were bagged at the scene and the body was removed by the Medical Examiner's Ambulance (R & R Conveyers, Inc.) and the door to the ambulance was locked at the scene by the undersigned.

The undersigned removed $97.00 in cash and a portable combination dial safe from the residence. A property receipt for the above items is on file.

TUESDAY, APRIL 7, 1981, 6:58 P.M.
SUK KU , residing at West Layton Avenue, phone 425- who is the minister of the deceased, came to this office to identify the body of the deceased. At 7:03 P.M., this date, the above-named individual, in the presence of the undersigned, identified the body of the deceased as that of CHUN SON Informant stated that about 2 to 3 months ago, the deceased told him that her husband was involved with another woman. Informant stated that he has known the deceased for the past 28 months.

JOHN L. O. JONES (SAS)

TUESDAY, APRIL 7, 1981, 7:30 P.M.
Identification Technician Leonard Karpinski came to this office and took six color photographs and gunshot residue tests of the deceased.

J. KORTSCH (SAS)

NOTE: Permission for gunshot residue tests prior to autopsy granted by Warren Hill, Deputy Medical Examiner.

Ribbed about crooked finger, teen kills self

MILWAUKEE COUNTY MEDICAL EXAMINER

CASE NO. 2006

SUPPLEMENTARY

Name TODD [redacted]
Date Death 10/18/78

Wednesday, 10/18/78, 11:15pm, Dr. Levine, County General Hospital, called and reported to the undersigned the death of TODD [redacted], white male, 14 years of age, born 12/31/63, of 2427A West [redacted], 643-[redacted].

He stated that the deceased had been conveyed to the hospital from his home by Milwaukee Fire Department paramedics. He was admitted to the hospital at 8:20pm, pulselss, non-breathing, clad in blue jeans, t-shirt, undershorts, black belt, tennis shoes, and white socks. Resuscitation attempts in the ER were somewhat successful and they produced some spontanious respiration, a pulse of 110, and slight reflex to deep pain. He was stabilized somewhat and was transfered to an x-ray table. There he arrested and at 10:50pm was pronounced dead. The informant stated that the deceased had sustained rope burns about his neck and that the staff had been informed that the deceased had sustained the injuries as a result of attempting to hang himself.

The undersigned then called District #6 and was informed by Sgt. Cameron that Squad 96R Early had investigated at the scene. He stated that he would have them call.

The undersigned then called and spoke with Detective Captain Joers. He stated that a detective team had investigated and he would have them contact this office.

Ptm. Boncel and Rehorst, Sqd. 96R Early, called and stated that they had been dispatched to the deceased's residence at 7:10pm this date to investigate a hanging. On their arrival they met several units of the fire department. The residence is a single family, two story residence with a raised basement commonly known as a polish flat. A portion of the living quarters are in the lower or basement level. That area consists of a kitchen, pantry, bathroom, and laundryroom. The officers observed the deceased on the floor of the kitchen receiving CPR from the firemen. He was clad as noted above and there was a multicolored shirt under him which the firemen had removed. The deceased was then conveyed to County General.

The officers notified the detective bureau and interviewed the family. They spoke with;the father, Richard [redacted], 12/28/40; the mother, Annette, 10/17/43; and sisters, Judith Ann, 4/10/67 and Brenda Lynn 3/7/71.

The eldest daughter, Judith Ann, stated that her brother, the deceased, had entered the basement area at about 6:30pm to exercise. He often lifted weights. At approximately 7:00pm she wanted a glass of water and entered the basement area. Moments later she looked into the laundry room and observed the deceased suspended from a water pipe by a length of clothesline. She then began screaming and Brenda joined her. The parents followed and the father lifed the boy while the mother attempted to remove the rope. Unable to do so the father removed the rope while holding the boy aloft. The mother stated that the rope from about the boy's neck was from the laundry room area and it was found that the rope had been cut from a loose end at the opposite end of the laundry room from where the deceased was found. The parents stated that the boy was situated so that his feet touched the floor, fully, with his knees bent. A chair was placed behind him, however, the deceased was suspended above the level of the seat. No books, magazines, or other paraphernalia was found in the area. The parents stated that the boy had not been depressed that they knew of and related minor incidents. They stated that about one month ago the deceased was involved in a fight in which his hand was broken. It was placed in a cast, which he removed prematurely. He found he had a crooked little finger and he received some kidding by friends. A specialist told the boy the condition was permanent and a second cast was put in place. The boy also removed this cast. The second incident involved the deceased telling his parents he was going to a movie with a friend and the friend's mother. The father learned that the boy had gone to a resturant with male friends and he restricted the boy's movements to playing in the house and yard for one week. This date the boy asked his father if he

3420

(OVER)

could go to the Boy's Club located across the street from his home. He was refused permission and the boy then played football with friends in the alley behind his home. He made no mention of attempting suicide, had no history or prior attempts, and gave no indication of depression according to the parents. The officers found no indication of anyone other than the deceased being involved in his death.

Detectives Schreiber and Repischka came to the medical examiners office and stated that they had investigated at the scene and concurred with the forementioned information.

J.R.Endrizzi

10/19/78 - 12:40 AM.

Went to the deceased's residence, 2427A West ████ Street and spoke with the deceased's parents, Richard ████ age 37, dob-12/28/40 and Annette Marie, age 35, dob-10/17/43, and the sister, Annette Cynthia, age 18,dob-6/21/60.

According to the parents; the deceased was a student at Walker Jr. High, in the 9th grade. The deceased has been a fair student, highly interested in sports and would spend much time at the Boys Club, participating in football, baseball etc., This past summer the deceased became involved with some boys who seemed to be trouble makers in the neighborhood. Nothing serious, that was ever proved, but enough to where the police would come to the house and check on the deceased's whereabouts. Nothing ever came of these escapades, but the father was cautious about where the deceased went and with whom. The deceased has been "grounded" the past week,(confined to the house and yard), because of telling the parents that he was going out to a restaurant with a friend and his parents, last week end, and the parents learned that he went with some of the"boys" instead. The"grounding" didn't seem to affect the deceased too much, since it wasn't the first time, and the deceased was able to go out in the yard and play ball .

On September 11,1978, the deceased was involved in a fight with a boy who was bothering a smaller neighbor friend. In the fight the deceased apparently struck the opponents head, breaking a b bone in the little finger of his right hand. The hand was placed in a cast. The deceased supposedly was being "ribbed" about the cast and eventually after three weeks, had pealed the cast off, necessitating a new cast . By this time the bones had knit to wher the bone had knit crookedly but it was too late to rebreak and the deceased was told the finger would be slightly misshapen. A new cast was put on, but the deceased removed this cast after a week. This didn't bother the deceased too much and he went about starting to lift weights in the basement as he always did.

The deceased was allowed to go to the Bays Club, last night, although who he went with,the father did not know.

Today the deceased came home from school at his usual time, went with the father and sister to pick the mother up from work at 4:30 PM, They came home about 5:00 PM, ordered some pizza, which they picked up and came home to eat. The deceased ate well and seemed normal . After receiving numerous phone calls from his friends, the deceased asked permission to go to the Boys Club. Permission was refused, so the deceased went out in the backyard and tossed a football around by himself until about 6:45 PM, then came back into the house. Shortly after the deceased went downstairs to the laundry room where he had a portion of the room set aside for his weight lifting equipment. Sometime later the deceased's 11 year old sister.Judith, went downstairs to the kitchen (Polish flat) to get a drink. The light was on in the laundry room. Judith lookedin on the deceased and saw him hanging by a rope around his neck, from the water pipe extending across the basement ceiling. She screamed to her father and sister who came down stairs and removed the body , from the hanging position. (the daughter that found the body was very upset and was sent to relatives for the night, so wasn't questioned.)

Questioned the deceased's 18 year old sister, Annette Cynthia, separately from the parents. A 16 year old brother of a friend of the deceased hung himself about six months ago. At that time the deceased stated "I'D never do anything like that".

(over)

MILWAUKEE COUNTY MEDICAL EXAMINER

CASE NO. 2006

SUPPLEMENTARY page 2

Name TODD RICHARD [redacted]
Date Death 10/18/78

The deceased wasn't too interested in girls. He supposedly had gone kind of steady with a neighbor girl last summer and was trying to go with another girl recently, but she didn't want to go out.

The deceased didn't have any money problems. He helped his dad in his roofing business and was paid for his services. She and the deceased would lift weights together, and just last night the deceased spoke of getting a bench for lifting weights. The deceased never drank nor did he use "pot". A couple of his friends did smoke "pot", but the deceased never did. He was always talking of becoming a football player.

The family physician is a Dr.Kostrzewski who saw the deceased occasionally, for minor illnesses. The deceased has been in good health.

The laundry room was checked, but all evidence of the hanging had been removed by the police. There is still a kitchen chair setting below the water pipe that extends across the ceiling. The ceiling is about 8' high. There is a set of bar-bells near the kitchen chair.

The family is at a loss to explain the deceased's actions.

E.Himmelreich EH

Thursday 10/19/78 at 9:55 A.M. Spoke with Dr. Kostrzewski, phone #383-1680, relative to medical history in the case of the deceased, Todd Richard [redacted], W/M age 14, born 12/31/63, and he related he has taken care of the deceased since January of 1978. The deceased had been treated for upper respirtaory infection, an injured knee, which he hurt playing basket ball, and a broken hand, which he had received during a fight. The deceased was never depressed nor was he suicidal in any sense of the word. The deceased was last seen on 10/4/78. Informant is at a loss for words,that would give rise to an explanation , as why the deceased took his own life . The deceased had a good home life and was always cheerful.

James J. Behrendt JJB.

3420

Window peeper falls from tree, dies

MILWAUKEE COUNTY MEDICAL EXAMINER

CASE NO. .1856.......

SUPPLEMENTARY

Name HARVEY E. ███████ W/M
Date Death 9/23/78

Saturday 9/23/78 at 8:40 A.M. Received a call from Dr. Laufenburg at St. Lukes Hospital, reporting the death of Harvey E. ███████ W/M age 47, born 2/12/31 of 13105 ███████ Road, Caldonia , Wi; whom he had pronounced DOA at 8:34 A.M. date. The deceased was conveyed from the rear of an apartment house at ████ So. Miner Street, by the Curtis Ambulance Service. A pair of binoculars was found adjacent to the body of the deceased and a limb from the adjacent tree had been broken off 10' from the ground and the police believe the deceased was window peeping. The body is cool and rigid, dressed in street clothes, and there is a slight abrasion to the bridge of the nose and some small lacerations to the forehead. Also that the body is being conveyed to the County Morgue.

9/23/78 at 9:15 A.M. spoke with officers Wayne Roberts and Gerald Francis, assigned to squad # 65 late, who related that they had investigated at the scene, ████ So. Miner Street, where the body of Harvey E. ███████ W/M age 47, born 2/12/31, of 13105 - ███████ Road, Caldonia Wi; had been found at the rear of the apartment building, about twenty feet from the building, at the base of a large tree, with a pair of Binoculars near the body. Interviewed at the scene was Mr. Robert ████, of 3854 So.██████ Street, Apt.#5, phone ████-0803, who related that he had heard some moaning about 2:30 A.M. but paid no heed, and about 7:05 A.M. date, his girl friend, Nancy ████ ,looked out the apartment window and saw the body of the deceased, and called it to his attention. When he reached the deceased, he found him to be unresponsive and then summoned the police. Miss Nancy████, born 2/10/40, related that she also had heard what seemed to be, a scream and then some moaning about 2:30 A.M.date, and just figured it was some kids acting up.
Interviewed was Miss Janice ██████, of 3858 So.██████ Street, Apt.#5, phone #████- 3057, who related that she had also heard some one moaning about 3:00 A.M. to 3:30 A.M. date, but went back to sleep and thought no more about it as the often hear noises during the night. She also related that she was in the habit of walking around in her apartemnt in the nude, with the lights on and the shades up, but never gave it to much thought, as the woods are next to the apartment. She further, related that she had noticed a Spector truck, driving around the apartemnts, quite a lot during the past week. The truck was being driven by a white male, but she could not say it was the deceased.
Interviewed at the scene, was Mr. Gary██████, born 5/17/56, of 3850 So.██████Street, phone █████-7455, residing in apartment #4, who stated that about 2:10 A.M. date, he had heard some one scream, but had not looked out to see where the scream had come from, as there was a lot of noise around the apartments at night.
Officers further, related that a limb had been broken off about ten feet from the ground , from the tree where the deceased was found. There were several pieces of bark from the tree near the body. They have the deceased's wallet, which contained $109.00 dollars, and numerous charge cards, drivers license, chaufers license, and numerous photos, of the deceased. Next of kin is the wife Sharon ██████, phone # 1-414████████, who has not been notified of the death .
Present at the scene, were squads, #65-L, 61, 64, 6, and squad #296, Officer Severson assigned , who took six photos of the deceased and scene. Also present were Detectives squads #112 & 106.
Officers also related that they had received numerous complaints of prowlers and widow peeping during the past two years, in that area. Further, that the deceased is supposed to have a farm truck, which they have not been able to find as yet.
All officers at the scene, believe that there is nothing of a suspicious nature so far as the deceased's demise is concerned.

9/23/78 at 9:45 A.M. spoke with Detectives Tomazewski and Zaporski, who related that they have noting to add to the report, and would like to be notified when Mrs. ██████ appaers at our office.

3420

(Over)

Saturday 9/23/78 at 9:50 A.M. The undersigned called the Racine Sheriff's office, phone # 8-414-636-3211, and requested they notify Mrs. Sharon Tougas, at 13105 -7½ Mile Road, Caldonia, Wi; phone # 835-2836, of the death of her husband, Harvey E. Tougas, and to have her call our office. They stated that it would be done as soon as possible.

James J. Behrendt J.J.B.

9/23/78 at 11:05 A.M. Received a call from Timothy [redacted], son of the deceased, and he began to cry upon learning his father Harvey was dead, as the Racine Sheriff's department had not informed the family of that fact. However he gained his composure and stated he and his mother, Sharon would be in our office this date, to identify.

9/23/78 at 11:10 A.M. Received information from Detectives Tomazewski and Zaporski to the effect that they had interviewed a Mr. Jerry [redacted] of [redacted] Highway (V) Franksville, Wi; Phone # 835-[redacted], presently employed at the Spector Trucking Company at 2040 W. Oklahoma Ave; as a mechanic, who related that the deceased, Harvey [redacted], had borrowed his 1978 Chevrolet, atabout 3:00 A.M. date, to check on something. The deceased had parked his mobile home acrossthe street from the trucking company, as he generally did, as he was a truck driver there, and his unit, was already loaded and ready to roll.
Further, that when the deceased failed to return at 7:00 A.M. date, he called the deceased's home, and was informed that the deceased nor his wife were at home. Mr. [redacted] then called the police.
Also intervived at the trucking company was a M . Ronald [redacted] operational manager, of 2205 E. [redacted] Drive, phone [redacted]-1103, who related that the deceased suspected that his wife, Sharon was cheating on him, while he was on the road, and may have been checking on her when he suddenly fell from the tree.
Detectives also related that some officer at the scene, had stated that the binoculars found near the deceased were the property of the deceased's wife, Sharon.

James J. Behrendt J.J.B.

Saturday 9/23/78 at 12:30 P.M. Mrs. Sharon [redacted], appeared at the County Morgue, and viewed the body of the deceased and stated that it was that of her husband, Harvey E. [redacted], W/M age 47, born 2/12/
She related that she and the deceased have been seperated since 9/1/78 because he was keeping company with another woman. She had moved into 3838 So [redacted] Street, inapartment #3, with a Miss Catherine [redacted] W/F age 22 and single, phone # [redacted]-5505 and does not know how the deceased obtained her address. She was not keeping company with another man. The deceased had beat her on occasions when he had been drinking. She had last seen the deceased on 9/21/78 at which time he had asked to come back to him as he was very lonesome. The deceased was not under a Dotors care and was not taking any medication to her knowledge. The binoculars mentioned in the report do belong to her and were kept in their trailer home.

James J. Behrendt J.J.B.

Natalie Wood

COUNTY OF LOS ANGELES

CASE REPORT

THOMAS T. NOGUCHI, M.D.
CHIEF MEDICAL EXAMINER-CORONER

3

Page 1 of 2

CONTINUATION SHEET

Case No. 81-15167

Case Name
WAGNER/Aka:WOOD, NATALIE

Found 11-29-81
Acc. 1
Date

Decedent is actress Natalie Wood who along with her husband Robert Wagner, a friend, and the skipper of the Wagner boat, were spending the weekend at Catalina Island.

In the early morning hours of Sunday, November 29, 1981, sometime after the group had returned to the boat, which was moered off the Isthmus, Mr. Wagner became aware that his wife and the boats dinghy were both missing. Mr. Wagner immediately radioed for help and a search was begun. Mrs. Wagner's body was spotted from the air by a Sheriff's Department helicopter that was enroute to the island to assist in the search. L.A. County Life Guards and two private searchers were the first ones to reach the body of Mrs. Wagner and pulled her from the water, where upon she was pronounced dead at 0744 hours.

Spoke with Don Whiting, night manager, of Doug's Harbor Reef, Catalina Isthmus, who related the following. Mr. Whiting arrived to work between 1600 and 1700 hours and the Wagner party was already in the bar and had been drinking. The party remained in the bar until approximately 1900 to 1930 hours at which time they were seated for dinner at the same location. During the course of the dinner, Mr. Whiting estimates that the group consumed a couple bottles of champagne. Mr. Whiting says the group left the restaurant to return to their boat at approximately 2200 to 2230 hours and that the entire group appeared to him to be intoxicated. Mr. Whiting at this time called Kurt Craig of the Harbor Patrol and asked him to make sure that the group reached their boat safely, which Mr. Craig is reported to have done.

Spoke with Mr. Wagner who related that the last time he remembers seeing his wife was at 2345 hours. Mr. Wagner when he realized his wife was missing, placed a radio call for help.

Don Whiting heard Mr. Wagner's radio call for help (Mr. Whiting lives on a boat and during his waking hours always monitors radio) at approximately 0130 hours and in turn called a friend on the Isthmus to go to the Wagner boat and advise him of the situation and if a search should be started.

When it was determined that indeed the dinghy and Natalie Wood were missing, a search was begun with Harbor Patrol, Bay Watch, private searchers, L.A. County Sheriff and U.S. Coast Guard all participating.

Mrs. Wagner's body was found approximately 200 yards off the Blue Cavem Point, Isthmus area of Catalina Island, and north of where the

INVESTIGATOR Pamela K. Eaker

DATE

WHITE - FILE
YELLOW - TOXICOLOGY
PINK - INVESTIGATIONS

76M118U - (REV. 4/73) - PS 11-80

COUNTY OF LOS ANGELES — CASE REPORT — THOMAS T. NOGUCHI, M.D. CHIEF MEDICAL EXAMINER-CORONER

3

Page 2 of 2 CONTINUATION SHEET

Case No. 81-15161

Case Name WAGNER/Aka:WOOD, NATALIE

Found 11-29-81

Acc. 1

Date

dinghy was found, near the shoreline, a couple hours earlier.

Mr. Wagner was also questioned regarding the possibility of suicide, however he states that wife was not suicidal.

Don Whiting was one of the private searches who located the dinghy and says that key was in the ignition, which was in the off position. The gear was in neutral and the oars tied down, and it appeared as if the boat had not even been used.

Decedent's body had been taken from the ocean and placed in the Hyperbaric Chamber building for safe keeping. Upon this investigators arrival at location, decedent observed lying in "stokes litter". Decedent is wrapped in plastic sheet, she herself is dressed in flannel nightgown and socks. The jacket that she was wearing when found floating, is no longer on the body, having come off when she was pulled from the water. At time decedent was pulled from the water, sheriff's personnel says that body was absent of any rigor and they noted foam coming from mouth. Decedent still has foam coming from mouth. Rigor is now present of a 3 to 4+ throughout her entire body. Decedent has numerous bruises to legs and arms. Decedent's eyes are also a bit cloudy appearing. No other trauma noted and foul play is not suspected at this time.

Skipper of the Wagner boat, Dennis Davern, identified body to sheriff's deputies.

Please notify Detectives Rasher and Hamilton <u>1-HOUR PRIOR TO POST AT 974-4341</u>.

PE

APPROVED. [signature] SR. INVEST.

Pamela K. Eaker
INVESTIGATOR
Pamela K. Eaker

11-29-81
DATE

WHITE - FILE
YELLOW - TOXICOLOGY
PINK - INVESTIGATIONS

76M118U - (REV. 4/73) - PS 11-80

Mom, 83, helps daughter in suicide

MILWAUKEE COUNTY MEDICAL EXAMINER

CASE NO. 1501

SUPPLEMENTARY

Name Elaine [redacted]
Date Death August 10,80

Sunday August 10,80 3:50PM Sgt. McKeown, district #6 called this office and stated that a body had been found at [redacted] W. Parnell, apt. #308. The officer requested an investigator be dispatched to the scene.

3:55PM The Medical Examiner's Ambulance and R.L. Goeb dispatched to [redacted] W. Parnell.

4:20PM The undersigned arrived at [redacted] W. Parnell, apt. #308 and was met by PO Anderson, squad #64, PO Debraska and Glapa squad #65 along with Det. Nowicki. The undersigned was directed to the bathroom of the residence which is located just inside the main entry to the residence. In the bathroom was the body identified as Elaine [redacted], DOB 5/6/27. The subject was dressed in a blouse skirt and stockings. The subject was seated in a wheelchair which had been backed into the bathroom. Abcut the subject's neck was a piece of yellow cloth. The cloth had been pulled through the eye of lift which was along side the bathtub and used to convey a person from a wheelchair to the bathtub. The boom of the lift had been raised to a point that with the subject's head through the cloth loop she would be slightly raised out of the wheelchair. Nothing further could be detected in the room relevant to the death. PO Anderson stated that he was called to the scene by Sophia [redacted], age 83, DOB 10/29/96, [redacted] N. Prospect the mother of the subject. The officer stated that as he responded to the scene Paramedic Unit #7 arrived and determined the subject was dead. The officer stated that he recalled being at the residence about a month prior to this time at which time the subject was on the bed threatening to take her life and stated that she had taken an overdose the day before. At that time the officer contacted some neighbors to assist the subject.

Today the officers were interviewing the mother at which time she informed the officers that her daughter had polio 30 years ago and has been confined to a wheelchair since that time. The subject was able to do some light work about the house and with the aid of the lift take a bath herself. The subject has become increasingly depressed offten threatening to take her life. Mrs. [redacted] stated that yesterday her daughter asked her to help her commit suicide. The informant stated that she refused indicating that she could get in trouble with the police. Today the subject convinced her mother that she would leave a note clearing her of all wrong-doing. With this the mother agreed to help. The mother stated that the subject took a piece of material and put it trought the eye located on the end of the boom of her lift. The subject than tied a knot in the material and placed the loop over her head and around her neck. The mother stated that she raised the boom enough that it lifted the subject off the seat of the wheelchair and left her. The mother than called for the police.

A note was found on the kicthen counter dated Aug. 9,80 and signed Elaine [redacted]. The note explains the subject's intentions and claims that Mrs. [redacted] is innocent of any wrong-doing. The note was retained by the officers for purpose of hadwriting comparison. The body was removed from the noose by the undersigned leaving the noose attached to the boom pending photos. The body was removed from the residence by the Medical Examiner's Ambulance.

PO S. Hall came to this office and took 3 photos of Elaine [redacted], DOB 5/6/27.

R. Goeb RLG

(OVER)

3420

(Cont.)

Monday, August 11, 1980: 10:00AM: Received a return call from Lorraine SCHMID, Medical Records, Milwaukee County General Hospital in reference to the medical history on the deceased, Elaine [redacted], age, 53. Informant stated that most of the information in the file will have to be subpoenaed. Informant stated that the deceased's history goes back to November 5, 1951 and most of them are emergency room visits. Informant stated that the last visit was on 2-11-78 for floaters in left eye. Informant could give any additional information.

William L. Harling WLH

Monday, August 11, 1980, 11:15 a.m.: Recontacted Lorraine Schmid, Medical Records, Milwaukee County General Hospital, in reference to a diagnosis of polio on the deceased, Elain[redacted]. Informant stated that on a summary dated August 8, 1973, the following is noted: "Past medical history of episode of polio in 1951 which has left her with almost complete paralysis of both lower limbs."

William L. Harling (ck) WLH

Man fatally shot in snow shoveling tiff

MILWAUKEE COUNTY MEDICAL EXAMINER

CASE NO. 183

SUPPLEMENTARY NO. 1

PAGE 1

Name GERALD ████

Date Death SUNDAY, JANUARY 21, 1979

SUNDAY, JANUARY 21, 1979, 8:15 P.M.
Debbie Nathan, R.N., called from St. Luke's Hospital to report that Curtis Ambulance conveyed a GERALD ████, 42, date of birth 3-17-1936, from ████ South 34 Street. Dr. Chudnow made the dead on arrival pronouncement at 8:00 P.M. Deceased is dressed for outdoors, the body is cool and limp and there is an entrance type wound located at the left side of the nose. Informant understands this is a homicide. Informant requested to place hold on body.

C. G. BORCHARDT (ss)

SUNDAY, JANUARY 21, 1979, 8:35 P.M.
Met at ████ South 34 Street, an older well-maintained bungalow, by Mrs. Dolores ████, 42, date of birth 1-7-1936, wife of GERALD ████, 42, date of birth 8-17-1936. She stated that they had been married for 14½ years and have lived at this present address for the past 9 years. Deceased is employed in the Sanitation Department of the City of Milwaukee. She said that he worked today on snow removal until his return home at 2:30 this P.M. After coming home, they went bowling during which time they had, 4, 5, or 6 beers and then returned to their home about 6:00 P.M. Mrs. ████ said that she and their 11 year old daughter went into the house while the deceased parked the car in the garage. She said she heard the neighbor's dog barking at the time. She said that deceased and a neighbor across the alley by ~~the~~ name of Kurt ████, who has lived there for the past 2 years, have been arguing over little things mostly since last summer. It seemed that the tension was building between them. Informant is not familiar with the circumstances. The police came to her and informed her that her husband was taken to St. Luke's Hospital. Deceased was in good health, was not under any doctor's care. The police had already left. Mrs. Nowak said her husband did not own a weapon. The shooting apparently took place in the alley area. It was initially assumed that Mrs. ████ was aware of the death but during the course of the interview, it became apparent that she was not. In the presence of the sister-in-law, Irene Dudech, phone number 671-████, the undersigned informed Mrs. Nowak that her husband was in fact dead and at St. Luke's Hospital.

9:25 P.M.
Contacted the Milwaukee Detective Bureau and spoke with Captain Walter Franklin. He said that the investigating squad, Billy Hacker, 112; Eric Pyczkowski and Pupero, Squad 101, are not presently available. However, informant understands that time of shooting was "6:45 P.M." location "Rear of ████ South 35 Street, in the alley". A .22 caliber, automatic was used which informant has not as yet seen. Distance of shooting was 3 or 4 feet. Assailant is Kurtis ████, age 27, of ████ South 35 Street. Informant stated that when the investigating squad has completed their report, he will have them contact this office with further details. Lieutenant Neuman of Squad 184 was also at the scene.

C. G. BORCHARDT (sas)

3420

(OVER)

SUNDAY, JANUARY 21, 1979, 10:05 P.M.
James K. [redacted], of [redacted] South 19 Street, brother-in-law to GERALD [redacted], came to this office and in the presence of the undersigned and Detectives Purpero and Pyczkowski of Squad 101, Mr. [redacted] positively identified the body of the named deceased. He stated that deceased was in good health and he last saw him this past Friday.

The detectives stated that a witness, Joseph A. [redacted], 41, date of birth 6-11-1937, of [redacted] South 35 Street, his wife, Carleen, and son, Joseph, were talking at the Lawrence residence with the deceased from about 6:15 to approximately 6:50 P.M. During this time, deceased had about 2 beers and took a third bottle with him as he left. He said that while deceased was at the residence, conversation concerned snow removal and the problems that the deceased was having with the neighbor across the alley, Kurt [redacted]. Deceased had gone to work at 5:45 this A.M. and got stuck in the alley. Deceased apparently had indicated that [redacted] had thrown snow onto his apron. Deceased had called the police because of this snow shoveling complaint. As the deceased was leaving the [redacted] house, they watched him through the door. [redacted] did not hear any argumentation but observed [redacted] fire a shot at the deceased. After the shot, [redacted] turned around and called to [redacted] to call an ambulance, "He'll need it." [redacted] mentioned to the detectives that deceased and [redacted] had been feuding since this past August. Another witness, Dennis [redacted], 20, 9-23-1958, of [redacted] South 35 Street, 672-[redacted], stated that he was out with [redacted] bowling this afternoon. They arrived home in their separate cars about 6:30 P.M. About 6:45 P.M. Dennis went outside to clear his part of the alley. At that time, he observed [redacted] shoveling snow in his area of the alley way. Dennis then went over to [redacted] and helped him shovel snow for about 15 minutes. In the meantime, the deceased came out of the [redacted] house, one door to the south, and walked up the alley way. Words were exchanged between the deceased and [redacted] while Dennis said that he continued shoveling his snow. He went on to say that he observed no blows nor did he observe any harsh conversation between the two. Dennis said he then observed the deceased follow [redacted] into the yard about 5 feet, Dennis being about 15 or 20 feet away from the two at the time. [redacted] and the deceased were facing one another about 5 feet apart. The deceased's left hand was in his pocket and he was shaking his right hand at [redacted]. Dennis said he heard the deceased say something about the cops coming. At that point [redacted] pulled a gun and shot deceased. Deceased initially slumped forward and then fell backward on the apron in [redacted]'s rear yard. Dennis said that he had not observed the gun prior to this incident. An empty casing was found about 12 feet west from where the shooting took place. The weapon was a .22 semi-automatic handgun, make of which is unknown to informants. One shot was fired. When the police arrived, [redacted] stepped forward to state that he had done the shooting and turned the weapon over to the police. He is now in police custody.

C. G. BORCHARDT (sas)
CGB.

10:30 PM - Sunday - January 21, 1979 - PO W.ERBACH, B of I, came to the Morgue and took three pre-autopsy photographs.

J.Kortsch JK

See Supplemntary #2

Poodle's stroke prompts owner's fatal attack

MILWAUKEE COUNTY MEDICAL EXAMINER

CASE NO. 627

SUPPLEMENTARY

Name ALEX ████
Date Death 3/26/79

Monday, 3/26/79, 6:40PM, Jean Sullivan RN, called from Trinity Memorial Hospital to report that the St. Francis Fire Department conveyed ALEX ████ 81, dob 8-16-97, from St. Francis Animal Hospital, being admitted at 3:53pm in process of cardio pulmonary resuscitation. CPR was continued to death pronouncement by Dr. Nunag at 4:38PM. EKG showed idio ventricular rhythyms with broad QRS, third degree heart block with cardio standstill with idio ventricular rhythyms resumed rate of 60 and extensive mycardio infarction damage. Deceased is dressed for outdoors, body warm and limp, no sign of trauma. Next of kin is a sister who identified the body but has since left the hospital. Her name and address was not recorded. Dr. Nunag has since left the hospital. Informant understands that the deceased was under care of Dr. Biller. Informant requested to have funeral director call this office before release of body.

6:50PM, Spoke with St. Francis Police Dispatcher Burgess. He said that investigation of ALEX ████ was handled by dayshift PO Heidemann. His report indicates that a Treacy Schultz, receptionist at the Animal Hospital at 3805 South KK, requested a squad. Deceased had brought his dog to the vet and, while in the office, the deceased experienced a dizzy spell followed by his collapse to the floor. Nothing suspicious is indicated.

8:25PM, Spoke with Mrs. Francis ████ 483-████, sister of ALEX ████. She said that her brother is a widower and has one daughter in a nursing home. Informant last spoke with deceased a couple of weeks ago and a brother, Albert ████, spoke with him yesterday with deceased making no unusual complaints on either occasion. However, deceased has a heart problem and emphysema but the name of the treating doctor is unknown to the informant. The informant will be at the deceased's residence tomorrow and will endeavor to obtain the doctor's mame and call this office. Deceased has had a poodle for the past 13 years and, today, it suffered a stroke while drinking water. The deceased then conveyed it to the vetnarian. Deceased had previously made the statement that if his dog died, that he would just as soon die as well.

C. Borchardt CB

Monday, 3/26/79, 7:15PM, Spoke with Dr. Biller who said that he hasn't seen the deceased for several years and does not recall diagnosis.

7:25PM, Spoke with Dr. Nunag who said that he saw deceased in the hospital earlier this date and feels that he suffered an myocardial infarction probably and will be willing to issue the death certificate.

C. Borchardt CB

Tuesday, 3/27/79, 8PM, Mrs. ████ called and said that she found the names of the following doctors at her brother's residence; Drs. Kesselman and R. Gussick. Both are elderly in high seventies. (checked phone director and found no listing on either doctor).

C. Borchardt CB

3420

Woman slain in sledgehammer attack

MILWAUKEE COUNTY MEDICAL EXAMINER

CASE NO. 434

SUPPLEMENTARY

Name RENEE NANCY[redacted]

Date Death body found Feb. 25, 1980

Monday February 25, 1980-7:10 AM - CAPTAIN THELAN, of the Milwaukee Detective Bureau advised this office, that the body of a woman, name age etc. were found in a garage at [redacted] West Fond du lac Ave. There is blood splattered about the garage. He requested that an Investigator and ambulance be dispatched.

7:20 AM - Field Investigator JOHN J. GUSS and the Medical Examiner's ambulance was dispatched.

J.T. Dubinski JTD

Monday, February 25, 1980, 7:50 A. M.: The undersigned arrived at [redacted] West Fond du Lac Avenue, which is a wood frame building with a garage about 70 feet to the rear and east of the residence. Met with Lt. ABRAMS and a number of other uniformed police officers and plain-clothes detectives at the garage of the residence. Inside the garage a body of a white female was observed lying on her back with her head to the south and feet to the north. The body was identified by Lt. ABRAMS as being RENEE NANCY[redacted], born: 4-7-53. The body is clad in levis and a blue, ski-type jacket. The levis are pulled down to the deceased's knees, with the panties also being pulled down to the deceased's knees. There is a section of a broom handle protruding from the vagina of the deceased. The arms of the body are limp. The exposed abdomen is warm to the touch. A rectal temperature taken at 8:20 A. M. was 60 degrees F. The ambient temperature was 23 degrees F. Also observed was the straw portion of the broom lying across the upper left chest of the deceased. A few feet to the right and rear of the head the 15 to 20 lb. sledge hammer was observed, with blood on the head of the hammer. The body appeared to have been moved because blood forms a semi-circle from the main garage door to the position of the deceased's head. There are two cars in the garage: a Pinto station wagon and a Datsun Hatchback. Deceased is lying to the rear of the Hatchback, which is parked face in. The Hatchback's rear door is open and a single key is in the lock. There are two gapping lacerations to the left side of the deceased's head. Parked east of the Hatchback is a Pinto wagon. Resting against the front of the Pinto wagon is a 4 ft. by 8 ft. piece of fiber board. Lt. ABRAMS said that the deceased's husband is a JAMES ALLEN [redacted], born: 12-11-52, and told officers that he had an argument with his wife, around 9:30 P. M., February 24, 1980. The argument was about the husband smoking cigarettes in the basement of the residence. The husband did not see deceased after 9:30 P. M., February 24, 1980, and, this morning at 6:20 A. M., he found deceased lifeless in the garage and called the police. The husband was taken to the Detective Bureau for further questioning.

R&R Conveyors removed the body from the garage to the county morgue at 9:10 A. M. this date, and the door of the ambulance was locked.

J. J. Guss JJG (slb)

Monday February 25,80 10:30AM PO Metzen BofI Milwaukee Police Department came to this office and took 2 photos of the subject Renee[redacted], age 26.

R. Goeb RG

Monday, 2/25/80, 11PM, PO Leonard Karpinski of the B of I, came to this office and took 3 full sets of finger prints and 3 black/white photos of RENEE NANCY[redacted].

C. Borchardt CB

3420

—OVER—

Tuesday February 26,1980; 2:05PM

Called the residence of the deceased RENEE ████ (353-████), but received no answer.

Thomas F. Hanratty

Tuesday, 2/26/80, 6:50PM, Ross ████ 31, dob 4-22-48, of ████ West Hampton 464████, came to this office and said that he is a brother to RENEE NANCY ████ 26, dob 4-7-53. Also present is Rochelle ████ 25, dob 10-4-54, of 4430 North ████ Street, ████ 6943, sister of the deceased. Rochelle said that she last saw the deceased weekend before this last and Ross said that he last saw the deceased last month. Deceased had no physical impairments except for vitiligo for about the past ten years. They were a close family and are at a loss to know who may have committed this act. They felt that the relationship between the deceased and her husband of the past seven years was normal. They viewed the body and stated positively that it was that of the named deceased.

C. Borchardt

Man dead in bizarre auto-erotic misadventure

MILWAUKEE COUNTY MEDICAL EXAMINER

CASE NO. 2 5 8

SUPPLEMENTARY NO. 1

PAGE 1

Name THOMAS G. [redacted]

Date Death BODY FOUND: MONDAY, JANUARY 30, 1978

MONDAY, JANUARY 30, 1978, 2:25 P.M.
Sergeant C. Hoppe of the 4th District Police Station called this office. Informant called to request an investigator and a conveyance at [redacted] North 98 Street. Informant stated that an obviously dead body had been found hanging at that address. The undersigned proceeded to the scene after dispatching the Medical Examiner's Ambulance (Community) to the scene.

3:00 P.M.
The undersigned arrived at the scene and was met by Detective McCue of Squad 104 and Police Officers R. Hanus and R. Neufuss, both of Squad 43.

The undersigned's attention was directed to the hallway within the upper flat at that address. The hallway in question connects the living quarters with the 2 bedrooms in the unit. One bedroom is positioned at the extreme east end of the hallway and another one to the southeast end of the hallway. The body of an adult white male can be seen in the hallway. The body is positioned with his back against the north wall of the hallway in a seated positioned. The body is nude. One end of a set of handcuffs is about the deceased's right wrist. The cuff is secured about the wrist. The other end of the handcuffs is positioned about the deceased's scrotum and penis. That portion of the handcuffs is also secured. There is a short coil of loose rope perhaps 2 feet in length lying at the deceased's feet. That rope may have been about the deceased's ankles and had fallen off. There is a nylon clothesline type rope fastened in a noose by a slipknot knotted about the deceased's neck. The portion of rope about his neck proceeds in an upward direction for approximately 3 feet at which point it passes through a pulley. This rope encompasses the pulley and continues upward to another pulley arrangement. The rope encircles this pulley arrangement and proceeds in a downward direction. The downward piece of rope appears to be approximately 10 to 12 feet in length and traverses beneath the door of the aforementioned bedroom positioned at the east end of the hall. From the position inside of the bedroom, the rope which ran under the door, can be seen to be wrapped about a barbecue skewer, the end of which is inserted within the small electrical motor designed to turn the skewer when it is in position on a charcoal grill. This electrical motor is plugged into a wall outlet and appears to be turning. The door to this bedroom had been closed when the body was found.

An examination of the body revealed it to be cool and somewhat rigid. There were no signs of life detected. The rope encircling the neck had left a deep leathery groove about the neck.

The deceased was identified to the undersigned as being THOMAS G. [redacted], 24 years old, date of birth 8-15-1953, and residing alone at [redacted] North 98 Street for the last 6 months. The deceased is a Laboratory Technician and has been employed for 5 years at the Autotrol Company located at 5855 North Glen Park Road, phone number 228-[redacted]. The deceased reportedly has a mother living at [redacted] North 98 Street, phone number 462[redacted]. The police had attempted to contact the mother but learned that she is at work. It was learned that the deceased had been at work on Wednesday, 1-25-78. He has not returned to work since that time. Today, a company representative and co-employe, Mr. Jeffrey [redacted] of 370 East [redacted], phone 483[redacted], came to the deceased's residence to check on his wellbeing. Being unable to gain any response he contacted the police department. At 1:45 P.M. Police Squad No. 43 arrived at the scene and forced open the locked door which had been chained from the inside to gain entry to the dwelling. The deceased was found as described

3420

(OVER)

above and the Medical Examiner's Office was contacted. Nine pictures were taken by the Police Department's photographer.

The dwelling was sparsely furnished but appeared to be in neat order. The deceased's wallet, containing some money, was found at the scene. There was nothing suspicious noted within the dwelling. Several empty beer bottles were found in the kitchen as was an empty quart whiskey bottle. No medications were found. The body was removed from the scene by the Medical Examiner's Ambulance. When the body was initially moved, the handcuffs' key was found under the body. Nothing was removed from the scene.

DAVID W. LIVINGSTON (sas)

Monday, 1/30/78, 9:10pm, Det. Stenzel, Milwaukee Police Squad 117, called and stated that he was currently at the home of Mrs. Deloris M. [redacted], 8/4/24, [redacted] North 98th Street, 462-[redacted].

He stated that she is employeed at Joe's Catering Service, and had not seen the deceased since 1/24/78 at 6:30pm. He had dinnerat his mother's home and was known to have no problems.

The undersigned then spoke with Mrs. [redacted]. She stated that the deceased had been over at her house for dinner and then had returned home where he was going to have a party with several of his friends. She stated that he should have been to her home for dinner on Saturday or Sunday night of this week but he had not shown up. She stated that this was not unusual and she had not become concerned. She stated that the deceased had attended Marshall High School and then taken courses at MATC in appliance repair. He had no history of involvement with the police and had no history of being involved in viloent or unlawful acts. She stated that he had been a good student, had no medical problems and had never been treated for of appeared to need the help of a psychiatrist. She stated that the deceased had never been the receipient of any threats from anyone. She stated that he had many male and female friends and had no particular girlfriend that he dated regularly. She stated that he had no money problems and was happy with his job. He had been living away from home for the past 2 years and had been living at his apartment for the past year. When asked about handcuffs she stated she knew her son not to be interested in police-type items and knew he did not have any such device. She mentioned that the officers informed her that the deceased had been caught in a pulley device. She stated that he had used a pulley device for the removal of an engine from his car and for lifting the car itself. She was informed that the pulley in question was not large enough to lift an engine or car. Further details were not volunteered.

The undersigned then spoke with Dale [redacted], 6284 North [redacted] 353-[redacted], who was at the residence and whom the mother had stated was the deceased's best friend. She stated they had known each other for many years. The subject [redacted] stated that he last saw the deceased about a week ago and that the deceased had never mentioned anything about taking his life, having problems with a girl, money problems, or any other type of problem(s). He stated that he did not know the deceased to have any type of erotic magazine or other publication. He did not know the decedent had handcuffs and did not know about the pulley arrangement. He stated the decedent was very normal in every respect and never mentioned bondage or masochism or intimated interest in similar sexual aspects. He stated that the deceased was very interested in mechanical devices and repaired eletronic and home appliances.

J.R.Endrizzi

Fetus unburied, found in cologne box

MILWAUKEE COUNTY MEDICAL EXAMINER

CASE NO. 2095

SUPPLEMENTARY

Name FETUS
Date Death 7/26/73

Monday, November 17, 1980, 2:05 p.m.: Milwaukee Police Department Detective Wolf (Vice Squad) Squad #107A, came to the Milwaukee County Medical Examiner's Office with a dirt-covered box believed to contain the remains of a fetus. The informant gave the following information: On, or about, July 26, 1973, a white female named Debra E. , age 23, DOB 6/19/57, of 2972A N. Street, phone 449 , had aborted a fetus at N. 33 Street. The above-named female was a run-away at the time of this occurrence. The above female, according to information received from her, had been continually sexually assaulted between the ages of six and 16 by a boyfriend of her mother's, named James P. , black male, in his 60's, N. 65th Street. In addition to this female being assaulted, the same black male had also assaulted, during this period, two other sisters. During the period of 1972 and 1973, the above female was living in an apartment at N. 33rd St. She was also having sexual intercourse during that time with a black male, Booker T. Jackson, in his mid 40's, who is since deceased. Informant stated that the above female was having stomach pains on 7/25/73 and continued all night into 7/26/73. The above male had gone to the bathroom at which time the clot came first, then the fetus. The above female did not know what to do so whe put the fetus in a plastic bag and went to see her sister, Marily , Dob 8/9/56, at an unknown address. She told the sister what hadhappened, at which time there was an argument because the sister wanted to take the fetus and tell her mother what had occurred. The sister then left to see her mother, at which time Debra hid the plastic bag containing the fetus in a stereo and left. Debra returned the next day, at which time she removed the plastic bag and had placed the fetus in a box marked "English Leather." She then went back to North 33rd and, using a spoon, buried the box containing the fetus in the back yard. Debra then turned herself into the Police Department as a runaway because she knew she needed medical attention, as she was hemorrhaging. The above information was concealed until 11/14/80, at which time she had been talking with her other sisters and had discovered that all had been sexually assaulted from their preteens into their teens by Bennett. Debra and her sister then went to the Police Department and reported the incident, who then turned the assignment over to the Vice Squad. Debra took Detective Wolf to North 33rd Street, at which time the box was recovered and subsequently brought to this office. The above female was present at this time and as such the undersigned interviewed same.

11/17/80, 2:15PM Interviewed Debra E. , white female, age 23, dob 6/19/57, of 2972A North Street, phone 449- , single. Debra gave essentially the same information as was given by Detective Wolf, stating that on July 25, 1973 (at the time she was 16 years old), she got severe pains in her stomach, which continued throughout the night into July 26, 1973. She had gone to an apartment that she was staying at, at North 33rd Street, and at approximately 12:05 p.m., on 7/26/73, the pains were worse, at which time she went to the bathroom. She stated that the clot came first, and then the fetus followed, which was dead. She further stated that she pulled the cord from the baby and herself, at which time the afterbirth came out. She then placed the fetus in a plastic bag and cleaned up. She then ran out of the house and went to a girlfriend's home (Rosetta or) (phonetic spelling), at 20th and Brown Streets, and told her what had happened. The man who she was having sex with at the time (Booker T. , deceased) was to be at that residence. Since he was not there at the time, and her girlfriend did not know what to do, she returned to North 33rd Street. At that time she set the plastic bag containing the fetus on the coffee table, and the landlord, who was present at the apartment at the time, told her that she could not keep it there and was to get rid of it. She then left and went to her sister Marilyn residence and had told her what had occurred. Her sister had been drinking at the time and they got into a fight over the fetus, about her sister going to their mother with the fetus to explain what had happened and who they thought was the father. Informant, who was a runaway at the time, did not want her mother to know, and when her sister left had subsequently hid the fetus in a stereo and left the apartment. She returned to the apartment the following day and had taken the plastic bag out and had placed it in a box and returned

#120

OVER

to 2755 North 33rd, where she buried same in the back yard, using a spoon. She then turned herself in to the Milwaukee Police Department as a runaway, knowing that she needed medical attention as she was hemorrhaging. She was subsequently taken to the Detention Home, and they sent her to Milwaukee County General Hospital, where a D&C was performed. Informant stated that when she told the hospital what had happened, all they said was that she should have brought the fetus with her. Informant stated that up until the first part of last week, she had not been aware that James P. ■■■■■, who was her mother's boyfriend, had, in addition to herself, been sexually assaulting her other two sisters from ages 6 through 16 years. After discovering this information, they decided they wanted to be charged against Bennett and had gone to the Milwaukee Police Department, who, in turn, sent them to the Vice Squad. Informant stated that at this time she is a welfare recipient and is going to school at MATC to be a computer programmer. She presently has two children with another black male, Henry ■■■■■, age 33, of ■■■■ North 36th Street. ■■■■■ is not aware of this incident. She further states that she wishes a proper burial for this fetus and was given the name of the Welfare Department burial clerk.

11/17/80: Talked to Elaine A. Samuels, M.D., Associate Medical Examiner, Milwaukee County, who examined the contents of the box brought to this office by Detective Wolf. It is determined that there are skeletal remains of a fetus of four months' gestation. The above information was given to Deputy Medical Examiner Warren B. Hill, who stated that the statute of limitation has run out, in this case, and he did not believe that charges could be made against the fetus' mother or the alleged sexual assault person named, James P. ■■■■■. He further stated that a case should be made. The fetus' mother, Debra ■■■■■, was shown the remains and stated to the undersigned and Deputy Medical Examiner Warren B. Hill that she wanted a proper burial to be done in this case and intended to contact the burial clerk at the Welfare Department tomorrow.

11/17/80, 3:20 p.m. Bof I Technician Richard Mazurzcak came to the County Morgue and took 18 black and white photos of the skeletal remains of Fetus ■■■■■.

William L. Harling (ck)

Vitals read:
AKA
Lenny Alfred Bruce

COUNTY OF LOS ANGELES
OFFICE OF CHIEF MEDICAL EXAMINER-CORONER

MEDICAL REPORT

Name LEONARD A. SCHNEIDER — Case No. 66-7907

Date 8-4-66 Time 38 — IN [X] OUT [ ] — Dr. Chapman

[ ] INVESTIGATION [X] AUTOPSY [X] PENDING [ ] FINAL ON

CAUSE OF DEATH:

ACUTE MORPHINE POISONING

Due to: INJECTION OF OVERDOSE

KEC:ag
Final: 8-12-66

Due to:

OTHER SIGNIFICANT CONDITIONS CONTRIBUTING TO DEATH

LABORATORY
- [ ] Micro.
- [ ] Neuro.
- [ ] Bact.
- [X] Photo By A.S.3 [signature]
- [ ] Date
- [ ] Toxicology
  - [X] Alcohol
  - [X] Barbs.
  - [ ] C.O.
  - [ ] Too Long for Alcohol
  - [X] Other—Explain Below

SPECIMENS SUBMITTED
Li K Stom Bile Ur Bl,

MODE OF DEATH [ ] NATURAL [X] ACCIDENT [ ] SUICIDE [ ] HOMICIDE [ ] ABORTION [ ] UNDETERMINED

Evidence of Injury [ ] Yes [ ] No Date ____ Time ____ A.M./P.M. ____ Describe: ____
at work [ ] Yes [ ] No

DATE OF OPERATION — OPERATION—Check One: [X] NO OPERATION PERFORMED [ ] OPERATION PERFORMED—FINDINGS USED IN DETERMINING ABOVE STATED CAUSE OF DEATH [ ] OPERATION PERFORMED—FINDINGS NOT USED IN DETERMINING ABOVE STATED CAUSE OF DEATH

MORTUARY M.E. CORONER - 8-4-66 @ 12:35 PM by Flowers + Vondra

Embalmed by: VONDRA License No. 3317 Blood Sample Taken [X] Yes [ ] No Crypt No. 14

Medical Evidence [X] Yes No [ ] Describe: SEE CONTINUATION SHEET — Clothing [X] Yes [ ] No

Embalmer's Observations: — Body Temp. NOT Taken By ____

Room Temp. ____ Time ____

PHYSICAL DESCRIPTION Age 40 Sex MALE Race CAUC Complexion MED Wt. 212 lbs. Ht. 71 In.

Hair BROWN Teeth U FAIR / L FAIR Eyes BROWN Pupils CONTRACTED Scars, amputations, beard old scar LT CHEST, old scar LT inside FOREARM, old scar RT inside UPPER ARM

Appliances on body ____ (Tattoo) or deformity LT FOREARM

Hospitalized [ ] Yes [X] No Hospital Report [ ] Yes [X] No Hospital No. ____ Unit ____

In ____ Jail Hospital Duration ____

For UNDETERMINED POSSIBLE OVERDOSE OF NARCOTIC

Other History RECENT ELICIT PUNCTURES BOTH ARMS

Supplied By SGT BERGER, SGT OSTEEN Hollywood Division LAPD. Address ____ Phone ____

Physician ? Address: ____ Phone ____

Diagnosis or Comment:

Information taken by F. H. Flowers

MEDICAL EXAMINER'S COMMENTS:
Hx of narcotics; multiple recent punctures.

Kenneth Chapman M.D.

76M118T-7-65

COUNTY OF LOS ANGELES
OFFICE OF CHIEF MEDICAL EXAMINER-CORONER

CASE REPORT

Tape # 3-37-B Start 600 End 602

Case No. 66-7907

Hospital No. ______ Crypt # 14 Taken by [signature]

Post Mortem at MEDICAL EXAMINER-CORONER Request of ______

NAME ~~[struck out]~~ LEONARD A. SCNEIDER AKA LEONARD BRUCE AGE 40 Sex M Race C Date and Time of Death 8-3-66 DOA 6 55pm

Place of Death 8825 HOLLYWOOD BLVD. HOLLYWOOD Pronounced Dead by 66 POLICE AMB

Reported by BERGEN Address HOLLYWOOD DET Phone ______

Date 8-3-66 Time 9:30 A.M. (P.M.) Phone at Scene ______

Police Investigation ☒ Yes ☐ No Police Agency AS ABOVE.

Officer ______ Date ______ Time ______ A.M. P.M. Supplemental Request ______

REPORTED AS:

- ☐ Natural
- ☐ Accident
- ☐ Suicide
- ☐ Homicide
- ☒ Undetermined POSSIBLE NARCOTIC
- ☐ At work

OVERDOSE ?

Residence of Deceased SAME Occupation ENTERTAINER Religion JEWISH

Employer ______ Soc. Sec. Number UNK. Military No. ______ Vet. UNK

Next of Kin KATHY SCNEIDER Address 1647 APPIANWAY SANTA MONICA Phone HO 98361
MINOR 10YRS LIVES WITH DECEDENT'S MOTHER SADIE KITCHENBERGER

Relationship DAUGHTER Notified by YES at ______ A.M. P.M.

Weight 212 lbs. Height 71 In. Hair BROWN Teeth U FAIR L FAIR Eyes BROWN PUPILS EVEN CONTRACTED Mustache YES + BEARD

Tattoo or Deformity LEFT FOREARM. OLD SCAR LT INSIDE FOREARM. Body Condition COLD FULL RIGOR MORTIS Prints ☒ Yes ☐ No Property ☐ Yes ☒ No

Brought in by FLOWERS + VENDRA Date 8-4-66 12 35 A.M. (P.M.) Door Sealed ☒ Yes ☐ No BUT NOT LOCKED

INQUEST ☐ Yes ☐ No Held on ______ Inquest Deputy ______

CERTIFICATE ISSUED: Pending ______ By ______ FINAL 8-12-66 By [signature]

REMARKS: SEE CONTINUATION SHEET

[signature: J. H. Flowers] Deputy

Assigned to Dr. ______

Pending–
FINAL CERTIFICATE By 8-12-66 [signature]

76C10884-7-65

Name: LEONARD H. SCNEIDER

Date: 8-3-66

CORONER
COUNTY OF LOS ANGELES
MEDICAL REPORT

Case No. 66-7407

Dr.

CONTINUATION SHEET

INFORMATION OBTAINED FROM SGT. BERGER, SGT O'STEEN HOLLYWOOD DIVISION LAPD.

DECEDENT WAS LAST KNOWN ALIVE AT 2^30 PM 8-3-66 WHEN HE WAS SEEN BY LILLIE ROMNEY.

AT 6^10 PM JOHN JUDNICK (SAME ADDRESS) CAME INTO DECEDENT'S OFFICE AREA - NOT SEEING DECEDENT HE STARTED WALKING OUT WHEN HE NOTICED THE SLIDING BATHROOM DOOR SHUT. HE CALLED TO DECEDENT NO ANSWER - SLID OPEN THE BATHROOM DOOR + FOUND DECEDENT IN A SEMISQUATTING POSITION ON HIS LEFT SIDE FACING SHOWER - PANTS DOWN AROUND ANKLES. HE PULLED DECEDENT INTO DOORWAY. WHILE DOING SO NOTICED BLUE CLOTH BELT AROUND RT. UPPER ARM. AND A HYPODERMIC SYRINGE WITH NEEDLE FELL TO FLOOR - IT WAS HIS IMPRESSION IT WAS IN DECEDENTS RT. ARM - POLICE AMB SUMMONED AT 6^41 PM PRONOUNCED DEAD ON ARRIVAL 6^55 PM. SGT BERGER REPORTED CASE TO M.E. CORONER AT 9^30 PM

DECEDENT LYING ON BACK IN DOORWAY TO BATHROOM - COLD TO TOUCH FULL RIGOR MORTIS. MULTIPLE RECENT ELICIT PUNCTURES BOTH ARMS (A.S.) ONE PUNCTURE RT. FOREARM BLEEDING. DECEDENT WEARING LEVI'S WHICH WERE DOWN AROUND ANKLES AND HUSH PUPPIES BOOTS UNDER DECEDENT'S LT. LEG SUIT COAT. WHICH CONTAINED BINDLE [illegible] WHITE MATTER - WRAPPED IN GREY PAPER - MEDAL BOX CONTAINING 11 SECONAL CAPS AND 11 MULTIPLE COLORED SPANSULE CAPS.

SGT OSTEEN WANTS POSSIBLE TURNIQUET + SUIT COAT AS MEDICAL EVIDENCE LEFT WITH BODY-

SEE MEDICAL EVIDENCE FOR MEDICATION FOUND + LOCATION OF SAME.

CALL SGT OSTEEN TO WIT. AUTOPSY HOLLYWOOD DIVISION LAPD.

ALSO REQUEST LAPD PHOTOGRAPHER TAKE PICTURES OF PUNCTURES.

F. H. FLOWERS

Name: LEONARD A. SCNEIDER

CORONER
COUNTY OF LOS ANGELES
MEDICAL REPORT

Case No. 66-7907

Dr.

Date: 8-4-66

CONTINUATION SHEET

MEDICAL EVIDENCE

1. HYPODERMIC SYRINGE WITH NEEDLE + CONTENTS ON BATHROOM FLOOR FOUND BY JOHN JUDNICK -
2. BOX OF WOODEN MATCHES IC ONE UNSTRUCK MATCH, 3 BURNED WOODEN MATCHES AND ONE BURNED CUPHER MATCH - FOUND IN BATHROOM
3. BOTTLE CAP (SOOT ON BOTTOM) FOUND ON TOP OF TOILET TANK IN BATH ROOM - WHITE RESIDUE IN CAP.
4. METAL BOX CONTAINING 4 WHITE PILLS AND 22 GREY PILLS FOUND ON BOOKSHIELF IN OFFICE AREA.
5. METAL BOX WITH 11 SECONAL CAPS AND 11 MULTIPLE COLORED SPANSULE CAPS, FOUND IN SUIT COAT THAT WAS UNDER DECEDENT (A.S.) FOUND BY VONDRA.
6. WHITE MATTER IN GREY PAPER BINDLE FOUND BY VONDRA IN SUIT COAT THAT WAS UNDER DECEDENT.
7. HYPODERMIC SYRINGE + NEEDLE FOUND IN JOHNSON'S STERILIZED COTTON BOX IN CABINET DRAWER IN BATHROOM.
8. BOTTLE IC 9 ORANGE PILLS FOUND ON BOOKSHIELF IN OFFICE
9. HYPODERMIC NEEDLE FOUND ON BOOKSHIELF NEXT TO PILLS ABOVE
10. ELGIN SYRINGE PAPER WRAPPER FOUND IN DESK IN OFFICE

ITEMS 1-THRU 4 + 7 thru 10 RECEIVED FROM SGT OSTEEN HOLLYWOOD DIVISION

11. SUIT COAT FOUND UNDER DECEDENT LET WITH BODY
12. BLUE POSSIBLE BATHROBE BELT AROUND RT UPPER ARM. LEFT WITH BODY POSSIBLE TURNIQUET.

F.H. FLOWERS

76M118U—5-58

Lenny Bruce

Information obtained from Sgt. Berger, Sgt. O'Steen, Hollywood Division, LAPD.

Decedent was last known alive at 2:30 p.m., 8-3-66, when he was seen by Lillie Romney.

At 6:10 p.m., John Judnick (same address) came into decedent's office area. Not seeing decedent he started walking out when he noticed the sliding bathroom door shut. He called to decedent. No answer. Slid open the bathroom door and found decedent in a semi-squatting position on his left side facing shower. Pants down around ankles. He pulled decedent into doorway. While doing do, noticed blue cloth belt around right upper arm and a hypodermic syringe with needle fell to floor. It was his impression it was in decedent's right arm. Police ambulance summoned at 6:41 p.m. Pronounced dead on arrival at 6:55 p.m. Sgt. Berger reported case to coroner at 9:30 p.m.

Decedent lying on back in doorway to bathroom. Cold to touch, full rigor mortis. Multiple recent elicit punctures on both arms. One puncture to right forearm bleeding. Decedent wearing Levi's which were down around ankles and Hush Puppies boots under decedent's left leg. Suitcoat which contained bundle with white matter wrapped in grey paper. Metal box containing 11 seconal caps and 11 multiple colored spansule caps.

Sgt. O'Steen wants possible tourniquet and suitcoat as medical evidence left with body. See medical evidence for medication found and location of same.

Medical Evidence

1. Hypodermic syringe with needle and contents on bathroom floor found by John Judnick.
2. Box of wooden matches with one unstruck match, 3 burned wooden matches and one burned gopher match found in bathroom.
3. Bottle cap (foot on bottom) found on top of toilet tank in bathroom. White residue in cap.
4. Metal box containing 4 white pills and 22 grey pills found on bookshelf in office area.
5. Metal box with 11 seconal table caps and 11 multiple colored spansule caps found in suitcoat that was under decedent found by Vondra.
6. White matter in grey paper bindle found by Vondra in suitcoat that was under decedent.
7. Hypodermic syringe and needle found in Johnson's sterilized cotton box in cabinet drawer in bathroom.
8. Bottle with 9 orange pills found on bookshelf in office.
9. Hypodermic needle found on bookshelf next to pills above.
10. Elgin syringe paper wrapper found in desk in office.
11. Suitcoat found under decedent left with body.
12. Blue possible bathrobe belt around right upper arm. Left with body. Possible tourniquet.

Woman falls to death in spat with boyfriend

MILWAUKEE COUNTY MEDICAL EXAMINER

CASE NO. 1677

SUPPLEMENTARY #2

Page #2

Name SUSAN [redacted]

Date Death September 10, 1980

4:20 PM - Wednesday - September 10, 1980 - ELIZABETH LUCK, M.D., County General Hospital, called this office and reported the death of SUSAN [redacted], age 25, single, a resident of [redacted] E. Curtis Pl.
Subject was brought to the hospital from a driveway at the residence.
Conveyance was made via Para Med unit #6.
Deceased had fallen or was pushed from a second story window at the residence.
She was unconscious on admission at 1:19 this AM and did not regain consciousness.
The admission diagnosis: "multiple trauma" specifically to the head.
X Rays to the head showed multiple head fractures. She also had C4 and C5 fractures of the spine and a probable fractured mandible. There was a small right subdural hematoma also.
Subject died at 4:14 this PM and the cause of death is due to the head injuries.
The above information was relayed to Detective Lieutenant G.WEISSMUELLER.
He said that a male friend of the deceased had visited with her yesterday evening and a drinking party ensued.
During the course of the evening, according to a witness, the male friend slapped decedent around and the argument culminated with deceased and the male friend falling from a window to the pavement of a driveway 16 feet below.
Detective Squad #107 is handling the investigation and will come to this office with the necessary information.
Medical Examiners' Ambulance - R & R Conveyors - called at 4:30 this PM to remove the body to the County Morgue.

J.Kortsch OK

6:45 PM - Wednesday - September 10, 1980 - Detectives SCHRODER and RILEY, Squad #107, came to the Morgue and relayed the following information:
Deceased is SUSAN [redacted], born 1-27-55, single, living in Apt. #3, [redacted] E. Curtis Place.
She lived there with a room-mate, one MICHELLE [redacted], 11-18-63.
A male friend of the deceased, one STEVEN [redacted], born 3-1-56, [redacted] N. 80th St., came to visit with decedent yesterday evening.
He had been drinking when he arrived at the apartment, exact time unknown to the informants. As the evening progressed [redacted] continued to drink and an argument ensued between the deceased and DeLaROSA.
He "slapped deceased around" according to [redacted] who was also present in the apartment throughout the evening.
At about 12:30 PM yesterday evening [redacted] was struggling with subject and they fell out of a window.
Deceased fell to the ground 16'7" from the window level of her apartment.
She reportedly struck her head on a parked automobile in the fall.
The officers have not interviewed [redacted] at this point but intend to do so this evening.
They have not as yet visited the scene to obtain a description of the window, etc.
The undersigned went to the Detective Bureau and obtained a copy of the report filed by PO J.MACHAJEWSKI and J.GRUENEWALD, Squad #14.
The report indicates the officers were sent to [redacted] E. Curtis Pl. at 12:30 PM on a complaint of a woman screaming.
They found the bodies of deceased and [redacted] along a north-south driveway beneath the second floor apartment of the deceased located on the southeast corner of the building.

3420

(OVER)

The report indicates ████████ was keeping company with ████████ up until a month ago. On September 9, 1980 at about 6:30 PM he came to the apartment bringing with him some steaks for dinner. He had been drinking when he arrived and continued to drink throughout the evening and engaged in an argument with the deceased. He began hitting her with the flat of his hand and then expressed his intention of taking his steaks and leaving the premises. Deceased blocked him when he tried to remove the steaks from the refrigerator. He struck her with the flat of his hand.
All three, deceased, ████████ and ████████, were standing near the window in question.
████████ tried to restrain ████████ from striking decedent.
████████ struck ████████ and knocked her to the floor. She hit her head against a metal table leg and was stunned for a few seconds.
She heard the crash of breaking glass. She got to her feet and noticed the window was broken. She looked out and saw the deceased and ████████ lying on the driveway below.
An automobile was parked on the driveway.
The officers think it was possible that subject struck her head on the automobile in the fall but had no physical evidence to bolster that belief.
The officers did not describe the window in their report.
Eight photographs of the scene were taken.
Detectives RILEY and SCHRODER will attempt to interview ████████ who is being treated for a broken neck at St. Mary's Hospital.
They are also attempting to contact ████████ for interview and said they will relay their findings to this office.

J.Kortsch JK

6:30 PM - Wednesday - September 10, 1980 - ID Technician J. VITRANO, B of I, Milwaukee Police Dept., came to the Morgue and took four black and white photograohs of the decedent.

J.Kortsch JK

10:40 PM - Wednesday - September 10, 1980 - Detectives RILEY and SCHOBER brought to the Morgue one JOAN ████████, ████ N. Woodburn, 332████.
She viewed the remains and made positive visual identification as those of her step-daughter, SUSAN ████████, born 1-27-55, single.
Mrs. ████████ had no knowledge of the circumstances resulting in the death of the deceased.

J.Kortsch JK

Thursday September 11,80 2:30PM PO Monfre came to this office and took 2 photos along with a right index print of the subject Susan ████████, DOB 1/27/55.

R. Goeb RG

Tuesday, 9/16/80, 12:05 PM: Contacted Dr Luck who said that she had checked the chart and dictation summary of SUSAN ████████ and could not find any lab slip or notation regarding a blood alcohol examination. Informant felt a test had been run.

John J. Guss JJG

MILWAUKEE COUNTY MEDICAL EXAMINER

CASE NO. 1677

SUPPLEMENTARY

Name SUSAN L. [redacted]
Date Death 9/10/80

#3

Tuesday, 9/16/80, 12:20 PM: Contacted Lavella Wilson, Blood Chemistry Dept, County General Hospital, who said there was no record on file for a blood alcohol test for SUSAN L. [redacted] on the 9th or 10th of September 1980.

John J. Guss

TUESDAY, SEPTEMBER 16, 1980, 9:45 P.M.
The undersigned proceeded to the Milwaukee Detective Bureau and reviewed the file relative to interview of STEVEN [redacted]. Detectives Gerald Kernan and Edmund Braun of Squad 101A Days interviewed [redacted] on Thursday, September 11, 1980, at 1:30 P.M. at St. Mary's Hospital Room 866. Their report is as follows.

STEVEN [redacted] stated that he was at the address of [redacted] East Curtis Place on Wednesday, September 10, 1980. He was with SUSAN [redacted] and MICHELLE [redacted] living at that address, Apartment 3, phone 224-[redacted]. He stated that they had been drinking; he stated specifically that he had been drinking wine and that he thinks that the girls had been drinking beer. He stated that he and SUSAN had gone out to pick up some beer earlier in the evening. We asked if he could recall the events that happened that night and he stated that he could. He stated that an argument had started in the living room of the residence and that MICHELLE [redacted] was struck and SUSAN [redacted] began arguing and told him [redacted] to leave the residence because he was no longer wanted and that he should get his meat out of the refrigerator. He stated that he went to the refrigerator to get his meat and MICHELLE [redacted] came into the kitchen and there was another altercation. He claims that he punched MICHELLE and that she fell down alongside the refrigerator and the next thing he heard was glass breaking, he turned around and saw SUSAN [redacted] falling through the glass in the window and he tried to grab her. He remembers falling through the window with her, but that is all he remembers after that. We asked STEVEN [redacted] how he thinks SUSAN [redacted] fell through the window and he stated that he thinks she fell over the beer cases that were stacked in front of the window. He also stated that he does not remember which part of her went into the window, whether she was facing front or backwards. He stated that when he reached out to grab her, he could not recall what part of her body he grabbed, but he does think that he did grab her.

C. BORCHARDT (SAS)

CB

3420

Boy dies after inhaling cooking spray

MILWAUKEE COUNTY MEDICAL EXAMINER

CASE NO. 1714

SUPPLEMENTARY

Name WALTER SCOTT [redacted]
Date Death August 24, 1977
(body found)

6:20 PM - Wednesday - August 24, 1977 - PO DALRYMPLE, West Allis Police Dept., called this office and said the body of a human being, sex, age, marital status, etc. unknown to the informant, had been found at [redacted] W. Washington. Medical Examiners' Ambulance - Meda-Care - called at 6:22 this PM to remove the body to the Morgue.

John Kortsch JK

6:45 PM - Wednesday - August 24, 1977 - The undersigned went to the residence, a single family frame ranch type structure at the stated address.
Met there with PO EVERSDYK, Squad #13, with Detectives KIRBY and PAVLETICH, West Allis Police Dept., and with WALTER [redacted], 42, resident of this address, telephone number is 774[redacted].
The kitchen of this dwelling is located in the southeast portion of the residence. On the linoleum floor is the body of an adolescent white male. The body is clad in a sweat shirt, blue jeans and jockey shorts. It rests in a prone position and favoring the right side with the head to the west, the feet to the east. The body is cold and completely rigid. It shows no obvious marks that indicate violence or injury on superficial external examination.
Mr. [redacted] identified the deceased as his son, WALTER SCOTT [redacted], born 8-27-63.
Also living at this address was deceased's mother DIANE and a 13 year old sister, CHERYL.
The father is employed with the [redacted]., Waukesha, Wis.
He left the house at 7:15 this AM to go to work. Leaving the home at the same time was his wife, deceased's mother, and his sister, CHERYL. The mother and the sister went to Edgerton, Wis. in order to set up their housekeeping arrangements in a camper they own there.
Deceased was in bed and presumably asleep when they left the residence.
The father returned home at approximately 5:30 this PM. He found deceased as above-described and called the West Allis Police Dept. immediately.
The father said he has had problems with deceased in the past, mainly of a minor nature. The only significant episode recalled by the father took place last May when deceased was found in an incoherent condition. Deceased admitted he had been spraying PAM, a vegetable coating, in a plastic bag which also contained his head.
The parents took deceased to a doctor located near N. 106th St. and W. North Ave., name and address not recalled by the father. This doctor counseled deceased for an hour but gave no further treatment.
Deceased was not a bad child but was ailing with "growing pains" and occasionally had to be admonished.
Yesterday evening the father and deceased had a spirited discussion in which the father remonstrated with deceased regarding his inattention to taking care of his chores and also discussed a sum of money which was missing from the home and could not be accounted for.
Other than that incident the father recalled nothing significant or remarkable that would aid in this inquiry.

(OVER)

3420

When the father arrived home he checked the living room and found on the floor in front of the couch a spray container of PAM with a plastic container for bread at one end of the couch. At the other end of the couch was a brown plastic garbage bag.
The father said that the can of PAM was not a normal adjunct to the larder, that deceased must have purchased it and kept it hidden from the other family members.
The only medical treatment deceased had of any seriousness was an appendectomy this past December, name of the doctor not recalled by the father. (The father was in a state of grief and could not readily recall such details).
He said the deceased was not suicidal and was never confined to any mental institution. He said deceased was of normal intellugence and was an average student at Lane Junior High School.
The father feels deceased sprayed PAM into a plastic bag with his head in close proximity to the fumes and his death is due to an accident.
The two plastic containers and the PAM container were brought to this office by the undersigned.
The PAM container label reads the contents are 13 ounces of a vegetable coating under pressure made of lecithin with a propellant (nature of propellant not defined).
The label bears a warning to the effect that deliberately concentrating and inhaling the fumes can be harmful or fatal.
The plastic container that at one time held bread appears to be ½ to 3/4 intact. It held Sentry thin sliced sandwich bread. There is a dried yellow residue within the bag.
Experimenting by spraying a small amount of the PAM on a piece of plastic shows the residue left is identical in color to that within the bag.
The garbage container is of dark brown plastic open at both ends and not otherwise remarkable.
The PAM spray can appears to be almost full.
The police officers said that among adolescents it is not uncommon to use PAM spray cans in a confined area and to inhale the fumes. By this method the user reaches a "high".
Deceased had never before come under the jurisdiction of the West Allis Police Dept.

John Kortsch JK

Thursday 8/25/77 9:25AM Doctor John Stuhler called this office regaring the deceased WALTER SCOTT ██████ DOB 8/27/63.
Informant stated that the deceased was brought in to his office on June 24 77, by his parents for useing PAM and a plastic bag and inhaling the fumes. Informant talked to the deceased and explained the dangers of what he was doing and warned him never to try this again. He also gave the deceased a phyical and found him in good health. Informant had nothing further to add but felt his talk had done some good.

J.K. Wollenhaupt

Man slain in dispute over socks

MILWAUKEE COUNTY MEDICAL EXAMINER

CASE NO. 1962........

SUPPLEMENTARY

Name Charles [redacted]
Date Death 10-28-79

Sunday, October 28, 1979: 10:40AM: Received a call from Det. JACOBS that a black unknown male was transported to Milwaukee County General Hospital from [redacted] North 24th Street with a stab wound through the heart. Informant stated that the transport was being made by Paramed # 6 from the scene. Informant stated that Det HAMBERGER, Squad # 113 is presently on the scene. Informant requested that an investigator meet Det HAMBERGER at the scene.

10-28-79: 10:41AM: Medical Examiners Investigator Robert SCHULTZ dispatched to the scene.

10-28-79:10:42AM: Received a call from Dr. WEBB of Milwaukee County General Hospital reporting a death.

Deceased is Charles [redacted], black male, age, 28, date of birth, 8-12-51, single. Informant stated that the deceased residence was 1323 West [redacted], phone unknown. Informant stated that the deceased had been transported by the above named Paramed unit from 1819 North 24th Street with admitting time being 9:09AM this date. Informant stated that the admitting diagnosis was Puncture wound to left chest. Informant stated that the deceased was pronounced dead by himself at 10:15AM this date with the final diagnosis being: Puncture wound, left ventricle. Informant was requested that he place a Medical Examiners hold on the deceased pending this units ambulance picking the deceased up for transport to the County Morgue. Informant had no information as to the circumstances.

William L. Harling WLH

10/28/79 11:05 AM At [redacted] N. 24th St. the undersigned met DET. A. ADAMCZEWSKI of Squad #118 and DET. D. HAMBURGER of Squad #113. They indicate that the deceased is a CHARLES L. [redacted], age 28, marital status not determined. Det. Adamczewski states that the deceased was temporarily living at [redacted] N. 24th St. He states that this morning shortly after 8:00 AM, the deceased got into an argument with TERRY [redacted], age 15, same address, over a pair of socks. He states that the argument went on outside the residence and up and down the block. He states that the deceased was stabbed in the chest by the accused in front of [redacted] N. 24th St. The body of the deceased had been conveyed to County General Hospital by a Paramedic unit earlier. The police diagram shows that the body of the deceased came to rest with head to the northeast and feet to the southwest in the southbound lane of N. 24th St. in front of [redacted]. He states that the knife has been found in a lot on the southeast corner of N. 24th St. & W. Vine St. The undersigned saw the knife which is an old kitchen knife with a wooden handle and a blade about 7" in length and 1" in width. The knife will be placed on infentory later after having been checked by the Bureau of Identification. He states that the assailant is in custody. He states that there are several eye witnesses now being questioned.

1:02 PM P.O. R. METTELMANN of Milwaukee Police Squad #37 came to this office and brought with him a WILLIAM [redacted], age 23, of 2710 W. [redacted] Ave., 933-[redacted]. At 1:02 PM, in the presence of the aforementioned officer and the undersigned, Mr. Woods positively identified the deceased as his cousin, Charles [redacted]. He states that the deceased lived temporarily at [redacted] N. 24th St. He states that the deceased had no home address and moved from cousin to cousin without establishing a permanent home. He states that other relatives are being notified of the death.

Robert E. Schultz R.E.S

Sunday, 10/28/79, 3:30pm, Ptm. Metzen, Milwaukee Police Department BofI came to the county morgue and took 2 black and white photos of the deceased, prior to autopsy.

J.R.Endrizzi

3420

Forced to study in Air Force, man kills self

MILWAUKEE COUNTY MEDICAL EXAMINER

CASE NO. 1299

SUPPLEMENTARY NO. 1

PAGE 1

Name MICHAEL STEVEN ■■■■

Date Death BODY FOUND: TUESDAY, JUNE 21, 1977

TUESDAY, JUNE 21, 1977, 4:50 P.M.
Ms. Taylor, Dispatcher, Hales Corners Police Department, called and reported that officers from her department were currently at ■■■■ West Parnell Avenue and that at that location, they had the obviously dead body of a white male. She requested an investigator to respond to the scene.

4:53 P.M.
Medical Examiner's Ambulance dispatched to the scene.

The undersigned drove to ■■■■ West Parnell Avenue and was met at the scene by Hales Corners Patrolmen Dorenbos and Jurkowski and Detective Hingiss. They identified the deceased to the undersigned as MICHAEL STEVEN ■■■■, white male, born 9-27-1959, with a Social Security number of 392-74■■■■. The deceased is the son of Harold E. ■■■■, 11-5-1922, and Bernice ■■■■ of the Parnell Avenue address, 425■■■■. The deceased is currently an Airman at the Chanute Air Force Base, Chanute, Illinois. The undersigned was then directed to the attached 1 car garage located to the west of the home and there observed a gold colored 1973 4-door Chevrolet bearing Wisconsin License plate GS ■■■■. Seen in the auto is the obviously dead body of the deceased. The head is to the west and feet are to the east. At this time, the passenger door is seen to be open and the hood is raised. The window on the passenger door is seen to be rolled down completely as the window on the driver's door. The interior of the car is much warmer than would be expected given the ambient air temperature and there is a marked heavy odor of exhaust fumes. The hood is warm to the touch and a large pool of water, appearing to be the contents from the auto radiator, is seen under the front of the car. The keys are in the ignition and the tank registers 1/4 full. The body of the deceased is clad in blue jeans, a sport type T-shirt, and what appear to be athletic type shoes of the Puma or Nike variety. The deceased's body is resting on its left side and the head is supported by a bed pillow.

The undersigned then interviewed Mr. Harold ■■■■ who stated that the deceased entered the Air Force on 3-15-77. He was sent to Lackland Air Force Base, Lackland, Texas for basic training. Following this 6 week period, he was transferred to Chanute Field for training as a welder. Following his transfer, he stated that his son had become very despondent. His son had been a rather poor student in high school and hated studying and books. His son complained to him that the Air Force Recruiter had lied to him and had promised him that he would not be required to study. The deceased complained bitterly that he was now forced to study and did not care for the Air Force because of this. On 6-11-77, the deceased came home and complained bitterly again about having to study. He stated that if he had to go back to the Air Force, he would commit suicide. The deceased's father stated that the deceased was nonspecific in his threats. He stated that he did not know that his son had not been allowed to come home on every previous weekend that he had been so permitted at that time. Mr. ■■■■ stated that on 6-13-77 he received a call from the deceased's Sergeant who informed him that the deceased was AWOL. At that time Mr. ■■■■ sat down with his son and talked over the problem at length with him. He then drove back to the Air Force Base with the deceased and had a long talk with the deceased's Major. The Major stated that the deceased had sometimes exhibited bizarre behavior, had been very despondent and had made threats against his life. Because of this the deceased had been treated at the Base Mental Health facility and had been kept there for several days on at least 2 occasions. Mr. ■■■■ stated that he felt the deceased's condition had improved and the deceased then stayed at the Base. The deceased drove to Milwaukee on 6-18-77 again spending the weekend with his parents. The deceased was last seen by his father between 11:00 and 11:30 a.m. At that

3420

(O V E R)

time Mr. [redacted] left the house and the deceased stayed with his mother. The deceased and his mother picked up various items of furniture from his grandfather's house and brought them back to their residence. They piled several chairs in the garage and at approximately 3:00 P.M. the deceased left to drive back to the Air Force Base. This morning, Mr. [redacted] left the house at approximately 8:00 A.M. for work. His wife left for work at approximately 10:30 to 11:00 A.M. to operate the tobacco store they run at the Parkland Shopping Center in Muskego, Wisconsin. Mr. [redacted] returned home at approximately 4:30 P.M. and heard a car running in the garage. He opened the garage door, which was unlocked, and found the deceased's car parked as noted above. He stated that the engine was running, the garage was filled with exhaust fumes, the passenger door was closed, and that he did not recall what position the windows were in. He stated he opened the passenger door, found the deceased in a lifeless condition and called for the police.

Officer Dorenbos stated that he was the first officer to arrive at the scene and that upon his arrival the engine had been turned off and the hood of the car to be raised. Mr. [redacted] later stated that he had not raised the hood on the car. Officer Dorenbos also stated that he then spoke with a neighbor, Theresa [redacted], [redacted] South 113 Street, whose house is located on a diagonal from the deceased's residence. She stated that she had been standing at the kitchen window doing dishes at approximately 11:00 A.M. and had noted a white car with a red top to be pulled into the driveway of the deceased's home. The occupants of the car then opened the garage door and removed a power mower. At that time there was no car in the garage. She stated that the 2 young men, who had been in the white car, then used the mower to cut the grass in front of the house and they then replaced the mower in the garage and left. Mr. [redacted] stated that the owner of the car is a Mr. [redacted], a friend of the deceased, whom he had engaged to cut the lawn during the course of the summer. Later in the afternoon, Mrs. [redacted] stated that she was again at the kitchen window at approximately 1:00 P.M. and at that time saw the deceased standing in the driveway with the garage door up. The deceased's car was parked on the driveway and the deceased appeared to be fanning smoke from the garage. She noticed nothing else and viewed nothing else relative to the deceased's actions.

Following the removal of the body of the deceased from the garage, the undersigned took Mr. [redacted] to the garage and he indicated that in order for the deceased to have pulled his car into the garage he had been forced to move an overstuffed chair, 2 folding chairs and at least 2 tires. These items had been piled to one side and were so situated that the door from the garage to the kitchen was completely blocked.

Officer Jurkowski stated that he had called the Air Force Base, 1-217-495-2809, and had spoken with the deceased's Sergeant, 1st Sergeant Robinson, who stated that the deceased had a roommate, William [redacted], and the deceased was last seen by his roommate at the base at approximately 9:30 P.M.

The undersigned called the United States Air Force Base, Chanute, Illinois, and spoke with 1st Sergeant Robinson. He stated that the deceased, MICHAEL STEVEN [redacted], was one of 500 of his students. He stated that when the deceased did not show up for his 5:30 inspection, he was declared AWOL this date. At 4:50 P.M. this afternoon, he stated that he called the deceased's father to find out if the deceased had returned home. He was then informed that the deceased had been found dead in the garage. He stated that the deceased had been declared AWOL on 6-9-77 and had returned on 6-13-77 with his father. The undersigned then asked the Sergeant if he knew the deceased well to which he answered "Yes". The undersigned then asked if the deceased had ever threatened his life and after a lengthy pause, the informant stated "Yes, he had threatened his life." At that point the Sergeant stated he

(CONT'D ON PAGE 3)

would make no further comment without official release of the information and official permission being given to him by his commanding officer or the legal counsel for the Base. He stated that the deceased had been treated at the Mental Health Clinic at the Air Force Base on several occasions and stated if the medical information was desired by this office, we should contact the Registrar USAF, Chanute Air Force Base, Chanute, Illinois 61668. He stated that no information would be given out by phone.

Also present with the Sergeant was the deceased's roommate, William ████, who identified himself as a white male, born 8-28-1956, and he stated that he had known the deceased for the past month. He stated that during this time he and the deceased had shared a common room and stated that he last saw the deceased between 9:00 and 9:30 P.M. He stated that the deceased had been to town last night and had returned to the Base. He was seen talking with a group of people in front of one of the Base buildings but according to ████, never returned to the room. He stated that this was unusual and that the deceased usually spent his evenings in the room when not visiting his parents. The undersigned then asked him if during the course of the past month the deceased had made any threats against his own life and after a substantial pause, ████ stated "No, the deceased never made any threats against his life." In the Investigator's opinion, the response was less than forthright.

Sergeant Robinson then came back on the line and stated that any additional information would have to be gotten by first contacting: Commander 3344 School Squadron, Chanute, Illinois 61668.

JAMES R. ENDRIZZI (sas)

Man in women's garb found dead in bed

MILWAUKEE COUNTY MEDICAL EXAMINER

CASE NO. 869

SUPPLEMENTARY

Name DONALD [redacted]
Date Death 5/5/79

Saturday, 5/5/79, 7PM, PO Cliff Kadow of the West Allis Police Department, called from [redacted] South 60th Street. Informant stated that an elderly gentleman, lifeless, is wedged into a hide-a-bed in such a position as to cause suspicion as to how it happened. Medical Examiner's requested.

7:20PM, Met at 1031 South 60th Street by PO Kadow of West Allis squad 12, Detective Barwick squad 81, additional uniformed police officers and David [redacted] 22, 1-24-1957, son of DONALD [redacted] 50, 8-21-1928. The deceased is lying face down across his bed with head to the west and feet to east. His head is wedged into the metal assembly of the lower folding portion of the bed. The left lateral neck rests on the rounded lower hinge with the upper metal portion snugly indented into the right lateral neck. Purge is emiting from the nares. The body is cool and rigid and is clad in ladies wear. The deceased's trousers are on the floor to the east of the bed, wallet is intact. Deceased's glasses are lying on the floor just ahead of his head to the west. There is an alarm clock tipped over just to the northwest of the deceased right hand, on the bedroom floor. The left hand lies along side the body on the bed. The panty hose appear to be undisturbed. There are several cigarette butts on the floor just off deceased's right hand. The bedroom is located at the northwest corner of the first floor residence. Both shades are down. There are numerous plants in the room. The room otherwise appears to be in order. The son said that the deceased has been divorced for the past three years and has been living alone at this address for the past year. Deceased is employed at the Schwaab Stamp & Seal company for the past 23 years and has a part time job as a guard. He was not depressed and not under care of any doctor, nor was he taking any medication. He smoked and drank but was not alcoholic. The son went on to say that the deceased was due to work this morning at 7. The deceased usually calls the son from his work or stops by at his residence after quiting. As the son neither heard from or saw the deceased today, he came to his residence. The residence door was locked and there was no response. All the house shades were down. He said that they are always up during the day because of all the plants the deceased has. The son opend the locked door with his key and found the deceased as reported at 6:45pm. A Roger [redacted] 61, 10-25-1917, of [redacted] South 83rd Street, 541-[redacted], came to the residence. He said that he and the deceased's x wife Lillian were at the deceased's residence from about 6:30pm to 7. [redacted] said that he always brings the deceased his weekly bus pass. All three are on good terms and the deceased was in no way depressed, being his normal self. Deceased had on his guard clothing at the time. Spoke with Frances [redacted] 72, who has been living upstairs for the past 10 years. She said that the deceased was a friendly person and never caused a problem. She last saw him about two weeks ago. The deceased's apartment consists of the bedroom, kitchen and bath. It was noted that there were red heart shaped pads on the floor of the bath tub. No medications observed anywhere. The residence does not appear to have been disturbed. The son said that he lives with his mother at [redacted] South 77th Street 327-[redacted]. He said that he never had any prior indication that his father may have been a transvesite. There did not appear to be anything suspicious. The residence was left in the custody of the son. The Medical Examiner's ambulance removed and conveyed the body with the ambulance door being locked by the undersigned. Two pictures were taken at scene.

C. Borchardt

OVER

3420

Saturday 5/5/79, 10:50PM, Spoke with Lillian [redacted], wife of DONALD N [redacted]. She said that deceased had emphysema from his heavy smoking but that he refused to quit. He also had broncho pneumonia. He has been treated at Woods VA, County Hospital, and had seen Dr. Wonder in the past. He also drank quite a bit but was not alcoholic. He was not depressed. They were on friendly terms. She last saw him last evening at which time he was sweeping his kitchen floor and made no complaints. Informant said that she would make funeral arrangements.

C. Borchardt

5/6/79 8:20 AM DONALD CZERNISZ, admissions officer at the Veterans Administration Hospital, Wood, Wis., returned a call from the undersigned. He states that he is unable to locate any record for a DONALD [redacted].

Robert E. Schultz R.E.S.

5/6/79 8:55 AM LORRAINE SCHMID, record clerk at County General Hospital, returned a call from the undersigned. She states that the deceased, DONALD [redacted], 8/21/28, had a record at the hospital dating back to 1965. She states that any information listed under inpatient or outpatient admissions at that time would require a subpoena. She states that the deceased was seen in the Emergency Department on 6/11/70 and 6/13/70 for a swelling of the left foot. Only diagnosis listed is rule out hyperuremia. She states that the deceased was seen in the Emergency Department on 6/22/71. She states that information under this admission would require a subpoena except for the fact that he complained of chest pain and that no rales were noted. She states that the deceased had not been seen at the hospital since 3/1/72 when he was seen in the Medical Clinic, no diagnosis listed.

Robert E. Schultz R.E.S.

5/7/79 2:10 PM Called DR. WONDER and was informed by his secretary that they have no record of treatment of the deceased, DONALD [redacted]. She states that the deceased's wife has been a patient of Dr. Wonder, but if the doctor had seen the deceased it would have had to be over ten years ago and that all such records are in storage.

Robert E. Schultz R.E.S.

Dorothy Stratten

FORENSIC SCIENCE CENTER
COUNTY OF LOS ANGELES

FORENSIC LABORATORY
GSR INFORMATION SHEET

THOMAS T. NOGUCHI, M.D.
CHIEF MEDICAL EXAMINER-CORONER

1314 FC-10486

82

- ☐ Probable Accident
- ☒ Probable Suicide
- ☒ Questionable Suicide/Possible Homicide
- ☐ Probable Homicide
- ☒ Homicide Investigator Requests Rush

☒ Male ☐ Female

INFORMATION ABOUT DECEDENT/SHOOTING

☐ Right Handed ☐ Left Handed ☒ Unknown

Occupation ____

Activity Prior to Shooting: Possible SEXUAL ACTIVITY

Have the decedent's hands been touched by anyone prior to taking the GSR sample (e.g., by paramedics, family, police, etc)? ☐ Yes ☒ No

If yes, by whom? ____

Was the weapon found in the decedent's hand? ☐ Yes ☐ No — Lying under hands, beneath body

If yes, which one? ☐ Right ☐ Left

Shooting Occurred: ☒ Indoors ☐ Outdoors ☐ Unknown

Location of Body: ☒ Indoors ☐ Outdoors ☐ Automobile ☐ Hospital

Other ____

Number of Shots Fired: Two

Date 8-14-80 and Time 1230/2345 of Shooting

Date 8-14-80 and Time 0345 GSR samples were taken.

FIREARM

☐ Revolver ☐ Semi-automatic/automatic ☐ Rifle ☒ Shotgun

Other (e.g., Derringer, Single shot pistol, etc.) ____

Made/Model: Mossberg Pump type Caliber: 12 gA.

AMMUNITION

Brand of Ammunition: Federal ? Type of Ammunition: #4 Buck, 12 gA.

Bullet Configuration: ☐ Round Nose ☐ Hollow Point ☐ Wad Cutter ☐ Pointed

Other ____

Bullet Surface: ☐ Jacketed ☐ Semi-jacketed ☒ Bare Lead ☐ Plated

Comments: SHOTGUN wound to head

M. Shepherd — Investigator 8-15-80 — Date

Do not write below this line

RESULTS:

Bullet wt: ____
Barrel length ____

White: Medical file
Pink: Laboratory Copy (to be returned to Coroner's Investigator)
Yellow: Laboratory Copy

76G8—PS 10-79

COUNTY OF LOS ANGELES

CASE REPORT

THOMAS T. NOGUCHI M.D.
CHIEF MEDICAL EXAMINER-CORONER

3

CONTINUATION SHEET

Information from Scene INVESTIGATION, And INV.'s OSTI, and DEANDA, AT Scene, 8-15-80.

Case No. 80 0485
Case Name
8 14 80
80 10485

Date

THIS NARRATIVE APPLIES TO BOTH CASES 80-10485 (HOOGSTRATEN) And 80-10486 (SNIDER)

Decedents ARE A 20 y/o Female and 29 y/o male, who ARE
MARRIED, BUT SEPARATED, pending divorce ACTION. Dec'd: 80-10485
IS THE 1980 PLAYMATE of the year (professional name: Dorothy STRATTEN).
Dec'd 80-10486 is her husband. Both are from VANCOUVER, B.C.,
CANADA. Decedents were living apart in the L.A. AREA. Dec'd
HOOGSTRATEN WAS STAYING WITH A MOTION PICTURE PRODUCER IN BEL-AIR
ESTATES. Dec'd SNIDER WAS STAYING AT THE APT. of A DOCTOR FRIEND,
DR. Stephen A. CUSHNER, M.D., AT 10881 CLARKSON Rd., W.L.A. Dec'd
SNIDER HAD HIRED A PRIVATE INVESTIGATOR, MARK GOLDSTEIN, TO follow
Dec'd HOOGSTRATEN.

According to occupants of the Apt. on CLARKSON Rd., and
the Private INV., Dec'd HOOGSTRATEN had agreed to meet Dec'd
SNIDER AT THE CLARKSON Rd APT. AT 1100 HRS, 8-14-80. The P. INV.
was following her at the time, and clocked her into the Apt. at
1230 HRS, 8-14-80. He then called Dec'd SNIDER, and reported this
to him. The other occupants of the Apt. had left, earlier in the
day. AT Approx 1900 HRS, 8-14-80, TWO Apt. occupants, PATRICIA LAURMAN
And LYNN (NPD) came home, and noticed dec'd's vehicles at the scene.
They saw the closed door, heard no sounds, and assumed Dec'd's
wanted privacy, so did not disturb the room. At Approx 1900/1930
HRS, 8-14-80, Dr. CUSHNER RETURNED, WAS told the situation, and did
NOT DISTURB the occupants. Note: LAURMAN and "LYNN" had been calling
Dec'd's Apt. since 1400, with no reply to the calls. At Approx 2340/
2345 HRS, the occupants became worried about the lack of activity from
the room. They called the Private INV. from the Apt., for a suggested
course of action. The P.I. told them to enter the room, while
he waited on the phone. They did so, and found both dec'd's
obviously dead, AT Approx 2345 HRS. They told the P.I., who told →

INVESTIGATOR [signature] CF2550 — DATE 8-15-80

WHITE - FILE
YELLOW - TOXICOLOGY
PINK - INVESTIGATIONS

Page 1 of 4

COUNTY OF LOS ANGELES

CASE REPORT

THOMAS T. NOGUCHI, M.D.
CHIEF MEDICAL EXAMINER-CORONER

3

CONTINUATION SHEET

Case No.
Case Name
8 14 80
54
80 1048

Date

CONT.
To call LAPD, and came to the
scene himself. Apparently the P.INV.
arrived prior to LAPD. LAPD WLA Ofcr.
HANNON observed both dec'd's obviously dead AT 0025 HRS, 8-15-8
Private INV. MARK GOLDSTEIN – bus. tele: 934-8666.

CORONER observed both dec'd's in a first floor bedroom
Both were unclothed, both in full rigor.

Decedent HOOGSTRATEN, 80-10485 was cool to the touch,
Lying semi crouched across the end of a low bed. There were live
black ants on the body, no maggots or flys. She was lying with
both legs on the carpet, and (R) shoulder on the carpet, with her
buttocks raised. SHE HAD BLOOD STAINS, possible HAND PRINTS, to her buttocks,
and (L) leg. She had trauma to both knees. She had an entrance,
close to contact shotgun wound to her (L) cheek, with much blood
loss. She had Lividity consistent with her position, set +4. She
had NON-CONSISTENT blood stains to her (L) shoulder and (L) arm.
There was blood splatter on the EAST wall and curtins, NEXT TO
her head. SHE HAD lost the tip of her (L) index finger, possible GSW.
beneath her was a towel, with a hole and blood stains.

NEAR Dec'd HOOGSTRATEN'S head, but at an angle away
from her, A "LOVE SEAT" SEXUAL APPLIANCE was on the floor. It
was set into a position for possible REAR ENTRY INTERCOURSE.

Decedent was Identified at the scene to LAPD by Dr.
CUSHNER, and verified by CALIF. Dr. Lic. for general physical
description. GSR TEST #1325 was done AT 0410HRS, 8-15-80.
Dec'd's Fingernail scrapings and hair samples were done AT
FSC. A SEXUAL ASSAULT TEST was requested by LAPD WLA.
Dec'd's apparent clothing was brought to the scene, from lying
near the bed. Note: the (L) slack leg was turned inside out, and
the blouse was turned inside out. The clothing was taken to
FSC by coroner. STRIPS of tape, both used and unused were
recovered from the room.

Michael A. Sleyster[illegible] 082580 8-15-80

INVESTIGATOR DATE

Page 2 of 4

WHITE - FILE
YELLOW - TOXICOLOGY
PINK - INVESTIGATIONS

COUNTY OF LOS ANGELES

CASE REPORT

THOMAS T. NOGUCHI, M.D.
CHIEF MEDICAL EXAMINER-CORO

3

CONTINUATION SHEET

Case No. 80-10[illegible]

Case Name [illegible]

[illegible] 8 [illegible] 80

HOMI

SEE ALSO 80-104[illegible]

Date

CONT.

Decedent SNIDER, 80-10486 was cool to the touch, lying prone on the rug, lying head to the ~~EAST~~, in line with the end of the bed. Live black ants were on the body, no maggots or ~~flys~~. He was lying with both hands beneath him, at lower chest level. A shot was observed under him, lying under dec'd, stock toward his neck, barrel toward the Ⓡ knee. ~~HE HAD AN ENTRANCE~~ SHOTGUN WOUND TO THE Ⓡ side of his head, with open wound between his eyes, and drain from the wound behind his Ⓛ ear. The Ⓛ eye was bulging from the socket. His Ⓡ HAIR HAD LONG BLOND HAIR IN IT (recv. by coroner in Misc. Evidence). The wound to the Ⓡ side of his head, had a blackened portion about it. GSR TEST #4314 was done at 0345 hrs. Dec'd's Ⓡ index finger was extended, with the res. the Ⓡ fingers curled. The fingers of the Ⓛ hand were curled. Lividity matched his position, to include an outline of the shotgun. He had trauma to his Ⓡ thumb. An expended rd. of 12 ga. #4 buck shot load, was recovered ~~from~~ the weapon, a 12 ga. Mossberg pump shotgun. It is 2'2½" from the depressed position of the trigger, to the end of the barrel.

An expended rd of similar type and an unexpended rd were recovered ~~from~~ the floor, about both bodies.

There was blood splatter on the west (closet) wall of the apt. Note: when the GSR TEST was done on dec'd there was some blood staining on both hands.

Decedent was identified at the scene, to LAPD INV's by Dr. Cushner, with general physical verification by Calif. Dr. Lic # N 6904418

Michael A. Shepherd #E8580 — 8-15-80

INVESTIGATOR — DATE

Page 3 of 4

WHITE - FILE
YELLOW - TOXICOLOGY
PINK - INVESTIGATIONS

76M119N - (REV. 4/73) - PS 7-79

COUNTY OF LOS ANGELES

CASE REPORT

THOMAS T. NOGUCHI, M.D.
CHIEF MEDICAL EXAMINER-CORONER

3

CONTINUATION SHEET

Case No.

Case Name

80 10405
HOOGSTRATEN DOROTHY
8 14 80
54
Date AUG 30 1980

AT THIS TIME, NO NOTES WERE FOUND. A TAPE RECORDER WAS CHECKED AT THE SCENE WITH NEGATIVE RESULTS. AT THIS POINT, NO ONE HAS COME FORTH WITH STATEMENTS OF INTENT OF ACTION OR ~~FRAME~~ OF MIND, OF VIOLENT ACTION, BY EITHER DEC'D, TOWARD THE OTHER DEC'D.

Dec'd's ROOM WAS SEALED WITH A P.A. SEAL, (THE SCENE APT.). Dec'd HOOGSTRATEN'S VEHICLE, A 1967 MERCURY, CAL. LIC "GALXINA" WAS LEFT LOCKED, AND LEGALLY PARKED AT THE SCENE, ON THE STREET.

Please notify INV'S. OSTI AND DEANDA, AT LAPD WLA, 1½ PRIOR TO AUTOPSIES ON BOTH CASES, AT TELE: 478-0731, EXT. 428

Michael A. Shepherd 8-15-80

Notified DEANA 0930 A/T 1030 8-16 80
[signature]

Page 4 of 4

INVESTIGATOR

DATE

WHITE - FILE
YELLOW - TOXICOLOGY
PINK - INVESTIGATIONS

76M110M - (REV. 4/73) -

Dorothy Stratten

Decedents are a 20-year-old female and a 29-year-old male, who are married, but separated pending divorce action. Decedent 80-10485 is the 1980 Playmate of the Year (professional name: Dorothy Stratten). Decedent 80-10486 is her husband. Both are from Vancouver, B.C., Canada. Decedents were living apart in the L.A. area. Decedent Hoogstraten was staying with a motion picture producer in Bel-Air Estates. Decedent Snider was staying at the apartment of a doctor friend, Dr. Stephen A. Cushner, M.D. Decedent Snider had hired a private investigator, Mark Goldstein, to follow decedent Hoogstraten.

According to occupants of the apartment on Clarkson Rd., and the private investigator, decedent Hoogstraten had agreed to meet decedent Snider at the Clarkson Rd. apartment at 1100 hours (11 a.m.), 8-14-80. The private investigator was following her at the time, and clocked her into the apartment at 1230 hours (12:30 p.m.), 8-14-80. He then called decedent Snider, and repeated this to him. The other occupants of the apartment had left earlier in the day.

At approximately 1700 hours (5 p.m.), 8-14-80, two apartment occupants, Patricia Laurman and Lynn came home, and noticed decedents' vehicles at the scene. They saw the closed door, heard no sounds, and assumed decedents wanted privacy, so did not disturb the room. At approximately 1900-1930 hours (7-7:30 p.m.), 8-14-80, Dr. Cushner returned, was told the situation, and did not disturb the occupants. Note: Laurman and "Lynn" had been calling decedent's apartment since 1400 (2 p.m.), with no reply to the calls. At approximately 2340-2345 hours (11:40-11:45 p.m.), the occupants became worried about the lack of activity from the room. They called the private investigator from the apartment for a suggested course of action. The private investigator told them to enter the room while he waited on the phone. They did so and found both decedents obviously dead at approximately 2345 hours (11:45 p.m.). They told the private investigator who told them to call LAPD and came to the scene himself. Apparently the private investigator arrived prior to LAPD. LAPD (detective) observed both decedents in a first floor bedroom. Both were unclothed, both in full rigor.

Decedent Hoogstraten was cool to the touch, lying semi-crouched across the end of a low bed. There were live black ants on the body, no maggots or flys. She was lying with both legs on the carpet, and right shoulder on the carpet with her buttocks raised. She had blood stains, possible hand prints, to her buttocks and left leg. She had trauma to both knees. She had an entrance close to contact shotgun wound to her left cheek, with much blood loss. She had lividity consistent with her position, set plus 4. She had non-consistent blood stains to her left shoulder and left arm. There was blood splatter on the east wall and curtains, next to her head. She had lost the tip of her left index finger, possible gunshot wound. Beneath her was a towel, with a hole and bloodstains.

Near decedent Hoogstraten's head, but at an angle away from her, a "Love Seat" sexual appliance was on the floor. It was set into a position for possible rear entry intercourse.

Decedent was identified at the scene to LAPD by Dr. Cushner, and verified by California driver's license for general physical description. Decedent's fingernail scrapings and hair samples were done at FSC. A sexual assault test was requested by LAPD. Decedent's apparent clothing was brought to the scene from lying near the bed. Note: The left slack leg was turned inside out, and the blouse was turned inside out. The clothing was taken to FSC by coroner. Strips of tape, both used and unused, were recovered from the room.

Decedent Snider was cool to the touch, lying prone on the rug, lying head to the east in line with the end of the bed. Live black ants were on the body, no maggots or flys. He was lying with both hands beneath him, at lower chest level. A shotgun was observed under him, lying under decedent, stock toward his neck, barrel toward the right knee. He had an entrance shotgun wound to the right side of his head, with open wound between his eyes, and drain from the wound behind his left ear. The left eye was bulging from the socket. His right hand had long blond hair in it. The wound to the right side of his head had a blackened portion about it. Decedent's right index finger was extended, with the rest of the right fingers curled. The fingers of the left hand were curled. Lividity matched his position to include an outline of the shotgun. He had trauma to his right thumb.

There was blood splatter on the west (closet) wall of the apartment. Note: when the GSR test was done on decedent there was same blood staining on both hands.

At this time, no notes were found. A tape recorder was checked at the scene, with negative results. At this point, no one has come forth with statements of intent of action or frame of mind of violent action by either decedent, toward the other decedent.

Decedent's room was sealed with a P.A. seal. Decedent Hoogstraten's vehicle, a 1967 Mercury, California license "GALXINA" was left locked and legally parked at the scene on the street.

Teen drinks to death in celebration

MILWAUKEE COUNTY MEDICAL EXAMINER

CASE NO. ...372.......

SUPPLEMENTARY

Name CHARLES [redacted]
Date Death 2/14/79

Wednesday 2/14/79 11:00 AM DR. R. CARDELLA called this office from County General Hospital to report the death of CHARLES [redacted], age 18, address not presently known to him. He states that the deceased was admitted to the hospital about six days ago via a Paramedic Squad. He states that the deceased had arrested and that he had been resuscitated by the paramedics. He states that the deceased was comatose on admission and had remained so. He states that the paramedics gave a history of blood on the face and in the nares of the deceased and it was assumed that he had aspirated something. He states that admission blood showed a .4 plus alcohol reading and that one drawn several hours later and registered .127. He states that the second one was done by Betadyne swab. He states that the deceased had been declared brain dead over a twenty four hour period and that the body and the chart had gone to the Pathology department so he had no other information. He states that the deceased's parents had signed a consent for autopsy. He states that cause of death pending autopsy is cerebral anixia - etiology undetermined. He states thatthe family telephone number is 562[redacted]. The undersigned then called the Medical Records Department at County General Hospital and asked that the deceased's chart be secured so that further information could be ascertained.

Robert E. Schultz R.E.S.

2/14/79 11:40 AM GAIL BUSS, record clerk at County General Hospital, returned a call from the undersigned. She states that the deceased is CHARLES [redacted], date of birth 1/27/61, age 18, of [redacted] N. Gordon Pl. She states that the deceased was admitted to the hospital on 2/8/79 at 11:07 PM having been conveyed to the hospital from [redacted] N. Warren Ave. by Milwaukee Fire Department Paramedics. She states that the deceased was comatose upon admission. Admission diagnosis was (1) Acute alcohol intoxication, (2) Pulseless non breather - resuscitated, and (3) Aspiration. She states that the paramedic report indicates that the deceased had been at a party at the above address, and that he had been drinking beer and amaretto and that he had been inhaling large quantities of marijuana. The paremedics notes indicated that there was valium on the premises. She states that the deceased was placed on the Byrd respirator while still in the trauma room and that he had been kept on it until being pronounced dead at 9:30 AM this morning by DR. CARDELLA.

Robert E. Schultz R.E.S.

2/14/79 11:55 AM Called the Milwaukee Fire Department Records Bureau and spoke with ESTHER FISCHER. She states that the conveyance of CHARLES [redacted] to County General Hospital was made by Med 5. She states that there report indicated that the deceased had been drinking beer and amaretto and inhaline marijuana. She states that there is nothing about Valium in the report. She states that Rescue Squad #1 was also on the scene.

Called Rescue 1 and spoke with FIREFIGHTER RONALD ULATOWSKI. She? states that when they arrived at [redacted] N. Warren Ave. an engine company had preceeded them and were giving CPR. He states that they took up resuscitative efforts until Med 5 arrived at the residence. He states that there were three other males at the residence and two uniformed police officers. He states that he was not aware of what the deceased might have ingested.

Robert E. Schultz R.E.S.

2/14/79 1:45 PM SGT. E.R. RESCHEL of the Milwaukee Police Department Detective Bureau returned a call from the undersigned. He states that according to the report filed by P.O. JOERS & KNEISLER of Squad #16 Early, they arrived at [redacted] N. Warren Ave. at 6:20 PM on 2/8/79. The report indicates that the deceased, CHARLES [redacted], was on the floor with firefighters working over him. The report indicates that they spoke with JESSE L. [redacted], 2/16/62, of [redacted] N. Warren Ave. who told they that they had been drinking beer and liquor for a long time. He told the officers that the deceased had passed out and that he had been unable to revive him so he called the Fire Department. There is no mention of any drugs in the report.

Robert E. Schultz R.E.S.

3420

(over)

2/14/79 1:55 PM Called County General Hospital and determined that the deceased, CHARLES [redacted], had been treated by a DR. STANLEY ATKISSON when first admitted. Called Dr. Atkisson who states that on admission he had blood drawn for alcohol only and got a reading of .454. He recalls ordering no other chemistry while the deceased was in emergency. He states that the paramedics had indicated that there had been liquid blood in the deceased's oral cavity when they had started intubation, but he states that all he actually saw was some dried blood in the nares.

Robert E. Schultz R.E.S.

WEDNESDAY, FEBRUARY 14, 1979, 3:45 P.M.
Contacted Police Officer Kneisler who said that on 2-8-79, he was working on Squad 16 and that he responded to [redacted] North Warren Avenue on a "Sick Person" complaint. At the scene he found a CHARLES [redacted], age 18, apparently lifeless on the floor with Firefighters working on him. The Firefighters managed to revive the individual and transported him to Milwaukee County General Hospital. He interviewed Jesse L. [redacted], 2-16-1962, who resides at [redacted] North Warren Avenue. [redacted] told the officer that the two had been drinking beer and a liquor. They were in conversation and [redacted] passed out. [redacted] added that they had been drinking together previously and [redacted] had passed out on other occasions that they have been drinking. [redacted] said that [redacted] had been passed out for about 20 minutes and he did not look right to him so he tried to wake him up. He could not get any response so he called for a rescue squad. [redacted] denied that the two were consuming any pills or drugs. Informant stated that he had contacted [redacted] mother and she informed him that he was not taking any medications at the time. The mother did not seem to be very concerned and was very reluctant to go to the hospital to make arrangements for her son. Informant said that detectives were not summoned to the scene and that they only filed a "Sick Person" report. He said that [redacted] lived alone at the aforementioned residence and that a younger group of kids hung around the residence and did a lot of drinking there. He said that [redacted] was shook up at the time of the interview and they did not ascertain how much beer and liquor [redacted] had consumed. There were no other witnesses at the scene.

JOHN J. GUSS JJG (sas)

Thursday, 2/15/79, 1:50 PM: Contacted Ora Simms, Pathology Dept, Milwaukee County General Hospital, who stated an autopsy was conducted on the remains of CHARLES [redacted] by Dr Paegle on 2/14/79. The findings were as follows: 1. Cerebral Anoxia and Infarct 2. a. Pnuemonia, severe, bilaterally, secondary to aspiration b. History of severe ethanol intoxication, blood level upon admission 0.454 Secondary: 3. Subclavian line in situ with hemorrhage subplurally and pectoralis muscle right side. b. Mediastinal & scleratal emphysema c. Drain tube insitu right plueral space 4. a. Status post nasal intubation b. Vocal cord tracheal mucosal erosion. The record did not indicate any trauma.

John J. Guss JJG

Friday, 2/16/79, 2:00 PM: Jesse [redacted] made a return call to this office and related that he was with CHARLES [redacted] on 2/8/79. He said deceased came to his house about 2:30 PM, 2/8/79, to celebrated informant's girl friend having a baby. He said deceased drank about 8 cans of beer and later drank ¼quart of Jack Daniels Whiskey in one swallow. Deceased appeared well when he arrived and did not appear to be high at the time. Deceased took no drugs nor did he smoke any marihuana. There talking together when the deceased passed out. Informant covered him with a blanket and later checked him at which time he observed deceased's face purple and called a rescue squad. He said the deceased has used marihuana before but no marihuana was used on that date.

John J. Guss JJG

Girl raped, slain after beer party

MILWAUKEE COUNTY MEDICAL EXAMINER

CASE NO. 1085

SUPPLEMENTARY NO. 1

PAGE 1

Name HEATHER ████

Date Death BODY FOUND: SUNDAY, JUNE 10, 1979

SUNDAY, JUNE 10, 1979, 2:15 P.M.
Received a call from Police Lieutenant Ed Bauer requesting that an investigator and Medical Examiner's rig be dispatched to the rear of ████ North 74 Street. Informant stated that there is an apparent white female body at that location.

2:20 P.M.
Medical Examiner's Ambulance dispatched and Medical Examiner Field Investigator dispatched to the scene.

2:40 P.M.
Arrived at 5020 North 74 Street and met with Detective Lieutenant D. Bottoni, Squad 157; Detective Riggle, Squad 107A; Detective Reichert, Squad 107; and Detective Hamberger, Squad 113; and Detective Maslowski, Squad 204.

The undersigned was directed by Detective Hamberger to the rear yard area of the above-named address where the undersigned's attention was directed to an area of bushes to the rear of this home. The residence is a brick ranch type home that faces west on North 74 Street. The body of a white female tentatively identified as HEATHER ████, age 15, date of birth 5-3-1964, of 7348-A West ████ Avenue. Informant Hamberger advised the undersigned that the above-named individual was reported missing from her home at 10:00 P.M. on 6-9-79. The body is found to be located 40 feet and 8 inches from the northeast corner of the home to the east. The feet are to the north and head to the south. The deceased's head is turned towards the west. A cursory examination reveals the deceased to be wearing one navy blue sock and a pair of white panties which had been pulled down to the right ankle. Deceased also is wearing a purple colored blouse. It appears there is blue-black discoloration to deceased's left eye with dirt in the oral cavity. There is a small amount of bloody material exuding from the oral cavity. It also appears that both upper arms of the deceased had been broken and the deceased, who is in a supine position, has her arms folded under the body. There were pieces of stick appearing to be pushed into the deceased's vagina. Informant Hamberger advised that the deceased's body was discovered by Mr. NOEL T. ████, white male, 37, of ████ North 74 Street, phone 466-████, at approximately 1:30 P.M. this date. Informant Hamberger further stated that the above-named subject and his wife, NANCY, had heard voices directly outside their bedroom between 9:30 and 10:00 P.M. on 6-9-79 and a female voice stating "I'm all right." It is also noted there is a small stick protruding from the rear portion of the right eye Photo Squad 297 with Police Officer Strang took numerous photos of the area. All items of clothing and money found at the scene were recovered by the Police Department and are on inventory. The undersigned locked the doors of the Medical Examiner's Ambulance at 3:40 P.M. this date. The undersigned then returned to the Medical Examiner's Office.

WILLIAM L. HARLINGER (SAS)

Sunday, 6/10/79, 5:00pm, BofI Tech Erbach came to the county morgue and there took 9 black and white and 4 color photos of the decedent, HEATHER ████.

Detective Paulous called and stated that at the time the body was removed from the scene he took a temperature reading of the soil and found it to be 59° F.

J.R.Endrizzi

3420

(O V E R)

SUNDAY, JUNE 10, 1979, 5:30 P.M.
Lieutenant D. Bottoni of Squad 157 and Detective Brown of 117 came to this office with MRS. SUSAN L. , 39, 10-20-1939, of 7348-A West Avenue, 462 . She stated that she is the mother of HEATHER ANNE , age 15, date of birth 5-31-1964, same address. Deceased is a freshman at Marshall High School and has no employment. She is not under the care of any doctor nor is she taking any medication nor does she have any physical impairments. They moved to Milwaukee from Eau Claire, Wisconsin 7 months ago. There are no other relatives in Milwaukee apart from a son, Peter, age 10, same address. The mother said that 9 months ago, the deceased was burned with a cup of tea causing some scarring to the left side of her neck and left shoulder and under the left arm. About 2 years ago, deceased underwent an interception of the bowel at the right lower abdominal aspect. Informant was aware of deceased having smoked pot but knew of no relative problems. Deceased never brought any boyfriends to the house and was not dating any. There have been no contacts with any previous friends from Eau Claire. She said that she last spoke with the deceased at 1:30 P.M. yesterday, 6-9. She told the deceased to stay at home and was not to leave the residence as the deceased was grounded for using her car without permission. Informant said she returned to the residence just after midnight and the deceased was not there. Her son, Peter, said that the deceased left about 7:00 P.M. to meet a friend called "SANDY NICHOLS" who lives on 71st and West Ruby. The deceased had mentioned that she expected to return home shortly. The informant's car was at home and had not been used. The deceased said she was going to Columbia Park at 72nd and Glendale to meet friends. Normally, the deceased's curfew on weekends was 11 or 11:30 P.M. but as previously mentioned, she has been grounded for the past 2 weeks. The deceased's grades had been slipping over the past 4 to 5 months but the informant felt that deceased had been pulling herself together once again with her grades improving slightly of late. The deceased was somewhat upset over the grounding. The informant said that she is a speech pathologist for the Milwaukee School System. Several weeks ago, the deceased had had a couple of cans of beer but otherwise she had no consistent drinking problem.

KAY , 14, 7-4-1964, of North 70 Street, 461- , said that she is also a Freshman at Marshall High School. She said that she last saw the deceased Friday at school at which time there was nothing unusual about her conduct.

In the company of the aforementioned police officers and the undersigned, the mother viewed the body and stated positively that it was that of the named deceased.

Lieutenant Bottoni stated that their department is presently involved in rounding up the party participants that SANDY mentioned having taken place at an address on 73rd and Hampton. Lieutenant said that their investigative information will be brought to the attention of this office when completed.

C. G. BORCHARDT (SAS)

Sunday, 6/10/79, 4:45PM, Contacted the Controller's Tower at Timmerman Field and spoke with Controller Jim Stanton. He stated that the 9pm temperature on 6/9/79 was 63° and at 10pm it was 60°. The overnight low was 59° with a 1pm 6/10/79 reading of 59°. 2pm temperature reading of 60° on 6/10/79.

C. Borchardt

Man kills self in store gun department

MILWAUKEE COUNTY MEDICAL EXAMINER

CASE NO. ..2005........

SUPPLEMENTARY

Name LANCE LANE ████

Date Death 10/18/78

Wednesday, October 18, 1978; 10:25PM, Dr. Shapiro called from the County General Hospital to report that a Para Tech ambulance conveyed an unknown white male, age about 21, from the K-Mart store at 76th and West Good Hope Road. Informant understands that deceased was witnessed by many in the store to shoot himself in the mouth. Informant made DOA pronouncement at 10:12PM. Body is fully clothed, is cool and limp. The head is bandaged. Informant requested to place hold on body pending authority from this office.

C. Borchardt CB

Wednesday, October 18, 1978; 11:40PM, Spoke with PO Tom Scholz of squad 45. He stated that he investigated into death circumstances of LANCE LANE ████ 20, dob 7-25-1958, of ████ North 107th Street. According to Linda Marie ████ 16, dob 4-27-1962, of ████ North Burbank 353████, a clerk at the K Mart store at 7401 West Good Hope, deceased came into the store at 9:15PM. Asked her if she had any 22 rifles. Asked if he could see the $42 one and if it had a safety tube. Miss ████ said that she didn't know. While deceased was taking the loader tube of the weapon, Miss ████ turned away to put some merchandise away. During this interval, she heard a muffled shot, turned and observed deceased fall over and bleed. The weapon is a Marlin Glenfield model 60 22 semi automatic. There was one spent cartridge marked Thunderboldt 22 long rifle. At no time did Miss ████ take out any ammunition. Deceased carried an ID card on his person with his picture. However, due to his condition, it was not possible to positively state that the picture was one and the same as the deceased. A record check was made with B of I showing file 168088, shows long record. Deceased 1972 Mustang Wis license X94-████, parked out on the store parking lot, revealed a box of similar ammunition. Miss ████ said that deceased gave her the appearance of being high on something and was chewing something. There did not appear to be anything suspicious. There may have been a witness which another squad is looking into. A squad was dispatched to residence.

C. Borchardt CB

10/19/78 - 1:50 AM.

Det.G.Bauer #104 called this office and states; he and his partner Det.G. Wank had brought the deceased's parents, Loyal L. ████, dob-1/6/29 and Lorraine L. ████, dob-8/4/28 to Milwaukee County General Hospital, where the father Loyal, after viewing the body, made positive identification of the deceased as that of Lance Lane, his son, at 12:02 this AM.

The deceased supposedly was having problems with his girlfriend with whom he was living at this time.

Eight live rounds of ammunition similiar to that used in the rifle were found in the deceased's auto.

E.Himmelreich EH

(over)

3420

Thursday, October 19, 1978, 9:55 A. M.: MRS. LORRAINE , North 107th Street, mother of LANCE LANE , was interviewed at her home. She stated that her son was employed by his father as a machinist at LOYAL MANUFACTURING COMPANY. She said he did not finish high school; he went as far as 10th grade. He had problems in school, both scholastically and emotionally. He would use intoxicating drinks and believed that he abused marijuana. For the past couple of years, he had been living with a Japanese girlfriend who lived at West Mill Road, Apartment 8. She said that her son did not come to their home very often. Last night, he came to the house and asked for some money because he wanted to buy a gun to go hunting with some friends on the following day. The parents did not furnish him with any money. He also indicated that he was having problems with his girlfriend and felt that he was depressed because of the problems. Informant stated that her son never attempted to take his life in the past, wrote no letters indicating he would take his life; never made any verbal indications he would take his own life. She said he was emotional, high strung and had a lot of anxiety. She said that, over a month ago, he had been admitted to ST.MICHAEL HOSPITAL for an infection. She said that his depression usually involved his feeling of inadequacy; that he was letting his family and his girlfriend down. She said he was handy, worked well with tools, but he would rather have worked at trades rather than the regular things that they taught in school. She said he had gone hunting in the past and believed that he was familiar with the use of firearms.

The deceased's aunt, MARILYN , was present and stated that the deceased was quick-tempered, never held a grudge and believed that he was getting medications from a DR. FOX. She believed that he used drugs and comsumed alcoholic beverages, and that she knew that he had had some kind of an argument with his girlfriend. Neither the aunt nor the mother believed there was any foul play involved in the death of LANCE .

The father of the deceased, STEPHEN , said that the son wanted money to buy a weapon the previous evening, to go hunting with some friends, but that he refused him the money. He said the son had gone hunting in the past and knew how to use firearms. He also felt that the deceased was upset over a disagreement with the deceased's girlfriend. The father said that the deceased never expressed any indications of taking is own life. The father did not believe there was any foul play involved in the death of his son.

October 19, 1978 - 10:40 A. M.: TAMIKO , date of birth: May 12, 1960, residing at West Mill Road, Apartment 8, was interviewed at her home. She stated that the deceased had been her boyfriend for two years, and that they were residing together. She said that, on many occasions in the past, the deceased indicated he would take his own life. She said, in the past, he had indicated he would take his own life by wrecking his car. She said,recently, the deceased had told her that she ought to go out and find someone better than him; that he felt insufficient; that he was inadequate for her and his family. She said that he had gone into depression on and off, but nothing in particular caused his depression; that it just came on spontaneously; and, on occasions, he was depressed butwould not display it to friends and neighbors. She last saw him yesterday morning before he left the house. She took $40.00 away from him because she felt he would spend it in bars. She did receive a call from him about 9 P. M. saying that he was coming home, but he never came, and that she went out looking for him. He never mentioned going hunting to her, or that he was going to buy a rifle. He had been treated in the past by a DR. GREEN and DR. LANGRAF of the Butler area, and he had received medications from a DR. FOX. She saidthe medications were chlorhydrate and Adevan. She said the deceased was a very hyper person and had trouble sleeping. She said that the deceased did not leave any notes indicating that he would take his own life. She gave an example of how he became depressed and stated that he applied for a loan to get a car, and the loan was turned down. It caused him to be so depressed that he punched a hole in the wall in their apartment. She said that he did not drink a lot of alcoholic beverages. She stated that hands used to shake a lot when he would get upset. She said that a DR. FOX had recommended the deceased see a psychiatrist, but the deceased never went to see him. She also said that he did not have any enemies, nor had anybody conveyed any threats against him. She did not believe there was any foul play involved in this death.

J. J. Guss JJG (slb)

Infant dies in toilet while mom tends bar

MILWAUKEE COUNTY MEDICAL EXAMINER

CASE NO. 1625

SUPPLEMENTARY

Name ALONZO ████

Date Death died 9/2/80

6:00 PM - Tuesday - August 26, 1980 - Captain FRANKLIN, Milwaukee Police Dept., Detective Bureau, called this office and reported the death of ALONZO ████, B/M, born 5-29-79, a resident of ████ N. Port Washington Road.
He said deceased's seven year old brother found subject in a toilet at the residence this PM.
The child was found dead by his mother who is a bartender in a tavern on the ground floor of the residence when she was alerted to the scene by the seven year old child.
On the basis of the above information the undersigned went to Childrens' Hospital where the decedent had been taken to meet with the investigating detectives.

At the hospital it was determined that the child was still in a living condition and was being taken to the ICU at this time.

J.Kortsch

Wednesday, September 3, 1980, 8:35 a.m.: At the Milwaukee Police Department Detective Bureau, the undersigned attained access to the technical report filed by the detectives J. Purpero and E. Tyczkowski on August 26, 1980. The report was filed into the injury of Quency Alonzo ████, DOB 5/29/79, of ████ N. Port Washington Road, Apartment #1. According to the report, officers spoke to Paramedic Parajecki who indicated that they responded to an alarm at that address at 5:04 p.m. The report indicates that, upon arrival, they found no life signs and started CPR and direct air resuscitation. The deceased was then conveyed to Milwaukee Children's Hospital.

The officers interviewed Curtis D████, 7/21/73, brother of the deceased. He told the officers that he and his younger brother were home alone. He told the officers he found his brother head-first in the toilet in the bathroom. The officer indicates that the floor of the bathroom was slippery ceramic tile. He indicates that the water closet was malfunctioning, causing the water to run continuously. A cursory search of the apartment indicated a small amount of old, moldy food in the refrigerator. It indicates that no other food, dishes, or kitchen utensils were found at all. The report indicates that the mother, Rose Marie ████, 3/12/56, had a bartender's license, and was employed at Sweet Jim's Taurus Lounge, ████ N. Port Washington Road, downstairs from the residence.

The officers then spoke with Crystal M. ████, 11/6/71, of ████ N. Pt. Washington Road, Apartment #2. She told the officers that she was in apartment #1 most of the afternoon on that date playing cards with Curtis ████. She told the officers that they cleaned up the cards. She told the officers she then asked Curtis, "Where's Quency?" She told the officers that Curtis said the deceased was sleeping, but that a check of the bedroom showed that he was not there. She told the officers that she then looked through the bathroom door and noticed the deceased, head down in the toilet bowl, feet in the air. She told the officers that she got her sister, Eva, and they ran downstairs and told Rose Marie ████ that Quency was dead. She told the officers that when they got back upstairs, the deceased was out of the toilet bowl, lying on the bathroom floor, and Curtis was looking at him. She told the officers that Rose Marie ████ picked up the deceased and undressed him and began pushing on his stomach and chest.

3420

The officers also spoke with Eva ████, 5/27/64, same address as Crystal. She told the officers that Crystal came to the apartment and told her that she thought that Quency was dead. She accompanied Crystal downstairs to notify the mother, and gave the same information as Crystal relative to finding the deceased on the bathroom floor with Curtis standing nearby. In addition, she told the officers that the deceased had white foam in his mouth and nose.

The officers asked Curtis ████ about the deceased being on the bathroom floor, and he told him that he had pulled the deceased from the bathroom bowl, and had just stood there and looked at him until his mother arrived.

The officer then spoke with the mother, Rose Marie ████, 3/12/56, and advised her of her rights. She told the officer that she had gone to work downstairs at noon on 8/26/80. She told the officers that she was tending bar until about 5 p.m. when Crystal and Eva ████ came downstairs and advised her that something was wrong with the deceased. When asked about arrangements she normally made for the children while she was working, she told the officers that the girl across the hall usually watches the children. When asked if any specific arrangements had been made for that particular day, she said, "No." The report indicates that the mother was ordered to appear in the District Attorney's office on 8/27/80 at 2 p.m.

R.E.S.

Robert E. Schultz (ck)

Student falls to death while shaking rug

MILWAUKEE COUNTY MEDICAL EXAMINER

CASE NO. 1418

SUPPLEMENTARY

Name BEVERLY A. [redacted]
Date Death 8-6-79

Monday, August 6, 1979, 8:40 A. M.: Received a call from Milwaukee Fire Dispatcher #14 (GRALINSKI) stating that they had an unknown female who allegedly had jumped from a window at 722 North 13th Street, and requested that an investigator and medical examiner's ambulance be sent to that location.

8:50 A. M.: Medical Examiner's rig; field investigator, William L. Harling, and Assistant Deputy Medical Examiner, David W. Livingston, dispatched to the scene.

W. L. Harling WLH (slb)

August 6, 1979, 9 A. M.: Arrived at 722 North 13th Street, which is a dormitory for Marquette University. It is observed that, in front of the building, which faces west, there is a body of an unknown white female appearing to be in her late 20's lying on the sidewalk. The head is to the north, and feet to the south; and there is a large amount of blood under the body. The Milwaukee Fire Department Rescue Squad #1 was in the process of removing the deceased to the County Morgue. Assistant Deputy Medical Examiner, David Livingston, contacted the medical examiner's office and cancelled the medical examiner's rig. The undersigned was then escorted up to Apartment 712 of the above-named residence and was met there by Police Officer EDWARD BESSLER, Squad #17, and Mr. JOHN CROSKERY, white male, age: 59, of apartment 111, the building manager. The above-named apartment consists of a bath, living room/ bedroom and small kitchen, which is on the southwest side of the building facing North 13th Street. It is observed that there is a screen out of the kitchen window and standing against the west wall just to the south of the window. The kitchen window has an upper and lower, with the lower being open. It is also observed that there is a spilled can of sugar on a small counter alongside the stove, which is located on the east wall; and there is also a warm cup of tea on the north side of the stove. There is also noted a small amount of sugar on the floor, with one side forming a straight line as if an object had been in place and had been removed.

The undersigned then spoke with Mr. CROSKERY, who stated that he had been working in apartment 701, which is just to the north of the deceased's. Informant stated that deceased is BEVERLY A. [redacted], age: unknown, who has lived in the above apartment since June, 1979. Informant stated that he had been working in apartment 701 since approximately 7:30 A. M. this date on the kitchen sink in preparation for renting the apartment. Informant stated that he had heard the radio playing and deceased talking on the phone to someone between the time of his arrival and the time of her death. Informant stated that, at approximately 8:30 A. M. this date, he had heard a "thump" and had looked out the west window and had observed the deceased lying on the sidewalk. Informant stated that he had run downstairs and had covered the body. Informant stated that someone unknown to him had already called the ambulance and Police Department. Informant stated that, when Police Officer BESSLER had arrived, they had gone to the deceased's apartment and had found the safety latch on. Informant stated that, in the presence of the above-named police officer, he had removed the screws of the above-named latch to gain entrance to the apartment. Informant stated that there had been no indication of a struggle. It was also observed that the entire apartment was neat and clean.

Spoke to Mr. CHARLES D. PAIGE, Public Safety Officer, Marquette University. Informant stated that theyhad received a call at approximately 8:38 A. M. this date of an unknown female who was lying on the west sidewalk at 722 North 13th Street, who was a possible "jumper." Informant stated that he had arrived approximately two minutes after the call and had observed the deceased in a position as indicated by the undersigned above. Informant stated that the Paramedics and Police Department had been called by an unknown person. Informant stated that he believed the deceased to be a law student at Marquette University.

An examination of the entire apartment indicates that there were no notes to indicate suicide, no sign of struggle, nor any medications.

3420

(over)

CASE NO. 1418

SUPPLEMENTARY

Name BEVERLY A. HEVEL
Date Death 8-6-79

Monday, August 6, 1979, 9 A. M.: The undersigned, along with Investigator William L. HARLING of this office, arrived at the scene at the Abbotsford Apartment complex, located at 722 North 13th Street. The building is a nine-story, multi-unit dwelling which houses Marquette University students and elderly residents. The following information is purely to supplement Mr. HARLING's investigation. Noted on the sidewalk in front of the apartment building is the body of an adult female. The body is positioned with the head to the North and feet to the South. The distance of the body from the building is approximately 11 feet. Posted over the entrance to the building is a canopy. The canopy protrudes from the building approximately four feet. The canopy is in line with the deceased's apartment window on the seventh floor. The deceased's eyeglasses and a rug, reportedly from the deceased's apartment, were noted on the concrete between the building and the body. The deceased was dressed in a housecoat, and no footwear was noted on the body nor near the body. Measurements in the deceased's apartment revealed that the window sill in the kitchen, through which window the deceased allegedly had exited, measures 33 inches from the floor level. The window sill is 14 inches wide. The actual window opening is 29 inches. As previously mentioned, it was noted that the full window screen had been removed and was pushed against the wall immediately to the south of the window. This screen is normally secured with two hooks on top and two latches on the bottom of the screen. The type of floor just under the window is smooth-surfaced tile covering. As previously noted, a warm cup of tea was in the sink, positioned approximately four feet east of the window. Some spilled sugar from a canister was also noted on the sink top. It was also noted that a small area of the afore-mentioned canopy, near the southwest corner of the canopy, had the dirt removed from it. Immediately below that area was some blood and bits of bone, indicating that some portion of the deceased's body may have struck the canopy before striking the sidewalk. Bits of broken blue-colored glass was noted near the deceased's body. It was also noted that the afore-mentioned eyeglasses had no lenses in them.

At the scene at the time was Mr. AL█████, 8417 West█████, date of birth: 6-7-10 (46█████). Mr.█████ stated that he is the parking lot attendant in Lot #6, which is located approximately one block immediately east of the scene. The lot is located at 13th and Wisconsin. Mr. █████ stated that, around 8:30 A. M. today, he noted an object falling from a high level in front of the apartment building. The informant could not identify the object and thought, perhaps someone had thrown something from a window. When the crowd started to gather in front of the building, informant proceeded to the scene and saw that it was a body that had been falling from the upper area of the building.

D. W. Livingston *dwl* (slb)

Tuesday, August 7, 1979: 8:35AM: Contacted Lorraine SCHMID, Medical Records, Milwaukee County General Hospital, in reference to medical history on the deceased, Beverly █████. Informant stated that the deceased was seen once in the out-patient clinic on 11-10-78 for severe sinus condition. Informant stated that the diagnosis at that time was " Allergic rhinitis since age 10. To be followed in allergy clinic". Informant stated that the deceased was given actifed # 60 at that time. Informant stated that the deceased was being seen in the clinic with no change in her condition but continuing the medications up to her last visit on 6-6-79. Informant stated that the record shows the deceased's problem to be under good control.

William L. Harling *WLH*

The undersigned checked the wallet of the deceased, indicating her name to be as above, with a date of birth of 12-3-50. A card placed in the wallet indicated an emergency number of a Mr. HAROLD RICHES, D.O. telephone: ███-5483. The card also indicates parents of the deceased: DONALD and BETTY ANN███████, phone: (616) 453-████. Police Officer GRAGE, Photo Squad 797, took an unknown number of photos of the scene. Assistant Deputy Medical Examiner David Livingston had taken measurements at the scene and had interviewed an eye witness during the period of the undersigned's investigation. The undersigned then took one black and white photo of the scene which is on file with this report and returned to the medical examiner's office.

August 6, 1979, 11:05 A. M.: DR. HAROLD KENNETH ██████, white male, age: 28, date of birth: 3-1-51, 622 North ████ Street (258-█████), husband of the deceased, arrived at the Medical Examiner's office and made positive identification of the deceased as: BEVERLY A.██████. The above-named doctor was interviewed by the undersigned, who states that his office is located at 3044 South ████ Street (545-████). Informant stated that he and the deceased have been separated since May 30, 1979 by mutual consent. Informant stated that the separation was due to differences pertaining to careers: his being medicine and hers being law. Informant stated that they had no children and had been married since August 19, 1972. Informant states that the deceased was a "women's-libber type" and had not taken his name when they married but retained her maiden name. Informant stated that the deceased worked at the Medical College of Wisconsin and has been taking courses at Marquette since their arrival in this state approximately three years ago. Informant stated that the deceased was to start as a full-time law student at Marquette University at the end of August, 1979. Informant stated that the deceased had not had any illnesses, other than some minor allergies: that she was taking a non-prescription medication for. Informant stated the deceased had been slightly depressed at the beginning of their separation. However, she had overcome this and was in very good spirits. Informant stated that the deceased works for DR. DANIEL MC CARTY at Milwaukee County General Hospital. Informant stated that he had last seen the deceased either Tuesday or Wednesday of last week, at which time she seemed to be very happy. Informant stated that they had made arrangements for the deceased to purchase an electric typewriter for her work at school, and she was going to go the end of the week to pick up her grandmother in Indiana so she could attend a retired nurses convention here in Milwaukee. Informant stated that they had separated on their own: and up to the time of the deceased's death, there had been no attorneys retained to pursue divorce action. The informant had no additional information to give.

11:35 A. M.: Contacted DR. Daniel MC CARTY, Chairman of the Medical Department, Medical College of Wisconsin, (7-6040). Informant stated, first of all, that he was extremely shocked at hearing the news, and that the deceased had been working for him for approximately 18 months now. Informant stated that the deceased had tendered her resignation, which he had accepted, to be effective August 24, 1979, so she could pursue a full-time career as a law student at Marquette University. Informant stated that there were no medical problems with the deceased, and that she was very happy. Informant stated that the deceased had no children. Informant stated that he had been called by the deceased between 8 and 8:30 A. M. this date, with the deceased stating that she was going to be late. Informant stated that he had last seen the deceased on Thursday, August 2, 1979, at which time she had left to take her grandmother to Michigan for a family reunion. Informant stated that the deceased had been working very hard trying to clean things up prior to her leaving on August 24, 1979. Informant stated that the deceased was a feminist-type who never changed her name after her marriage to DR.██████. Informant stated that, to his knowledge, the deceased had never attempted to take her life, nor was she ever depressed, to his knowledge. Informant had no additional information to give.

William L. Harling WLH (slb)

Note: It is noted here that there is a small rug similar to one in the deceased's apt. which is on the sidewalk alongside of the body when observed.

Monday, August 6, 1979: Contacted Melanie at Medical Records, Deaconess Hospital in reference to any medical history on the deceased, Beverly A. █████. Informant stated that a check of their records show that the deceased has not been seen at that hospital.

Minday, August 6, 1979: 2:00PM Contacted Lorraine SCHMID, Medical Records, Milwaukee County General Hospital, in reference to any medical history on the deceased, Beverly A.█████. Informant stated that they have one out-patient visit and that she will pull the record and call back

Wednesday, August 8, 1979, 8:40 A. M.: MRS. MAX ████████, 4419 North Prospect Avenue (964-█████), called this office. Informant stated that her husband, MAX, may have some additional information regarding the death of BEVERLY █████. Informant stated that her husband can be reached after 9 A. M. today at 547-█████.

9:25 A. M.: The undersigned contacted MAX ████████ at the above-listed number. The informant is the proprietor of the Main Street Arts Store located at 336 West Main Street, Waukesha, WI. Informant related that, on Monday, August 6, 1979, at approximately 8 A. M., he was making a delivery to Marquette University's Book Store located on North 13th Street and West Wisconsin Avenue. Informant added that, in order to make a delivery, he had to back into a loading dock which is located on the west side of North 13th Street near Wisconsin Avenue. In so doing, his vehicle faced north. He had an unobstructed view in a northeast direction. Informant added that, between 8 A. M. and 8:15 A. M., he was seated in his automobile. At 8:15 A. M., he left his vehicle and entered the building. At about 8:25 A. M., he returned to his vehicle and left the area. Informant stated that, while he was seated in his automobile between 8 and 8:15 A. M., he noted a young-appearing white female shaking a rug out of a window in the apartment building located at 722 North 13th Street. Informant thinks it may have been a 6th or 7th-story window. Informant had never seen the woman before. He could not give a description of the subject, but thinks she may have had dark hair and an orange-colored dress on. While watching the woman shake the rug, informant became alarmed because she appeared to be leaning much too far out of the window for safety sake. Informant noted that the woman appeared to be shaking a small rug. Informant also observed that she did this at least four - and perhaps five - separate occasions during the 15 minutes that he was there. Each time she shook the rug, it appeared to be the same one. Each time she shook the rug, she appeared to lean much, much to far out of the window for safety sake. Informant added that he had not been in that area for at least six months prior to August 6, 1979. Informant did not personally know, nor had he even heard of, BEVERLY █████ other than reading about the incident in the newspapers.

D. W. Livingston *DWL* (slb)

Freddie Prinze

COUNTY OF LOS ANGELES

CASE REPORT

THOMAS T. NOGUCHI, M.D.
CHIEF MEDICAL EXAMINER-CORONER

3

CONTINUATION SHEET

Case No.
Case Name
PRINZE FREDDIE
[illegible] 1-29-77
SUICIDE 94
Date

Information obtained from Sgt. Kinard W.L.A.P.D. and U.C.L.A. Hospital death report.

The decedent is a 22 year old male who has been despondent for the past several weeks over work and marital problems. The decedent was in the process of a divorce and had mentioned several times that "I should end it all", meaning that he should take his own life. During the past few days the decedent had in his possession a 38 cal. revolver which he had been toying with. Loading it and unloading it. On 1-28-77 the decedent was with his secretary and was once again toying with the gun and asked her to contact Dr. Craiger, who is the decedents psychologist; he talked with the decedent for a short time and hungup. A Mr. Marvin Snyder was present with the decedent on 1-28-77 and at the time the decedent was going through a stage of extreme depression, as discribed by, business manager Marvin Snyder. At 0330 hrs 1-28-77 the decedent called his wife and they talked a few minutes over the phone and he informed her that he was going to end it all. The decedent hung the phone up and held the revolver to his head and shot himself. A rescue ambulance was summoned and the decedent was transported to the above hospital where he underwent surgery for a G.S.W. to the head. T & T. The decedents condition never improved and on 1-29-77 at 1300 hrs Dr. C.M. Hyshaw pronounced death.

A projectile was recovered by W.L.A. Division and a suicide note was also taken by the above investigating agency. The decedent had apparently test fired the gun recently or accidently fired it while toying with it. A projectile was recovered in another room which revealed that it was a recent shot fired, due to small amount of debris in the area. S.I.D. Central Division took the gun in for prints.

A suicide note dated 1-28-77 was also taken by Det. Rosenbrock. Note was brief and only stated that he was ending it all and that the man present had nothing to do with his death.

ID by body tag

Death report will be forwarded to this department.

[signature] INVESTIGATOR 1-29-77 DATE

WHITE - FILE
YELLOW - TOXICOLOGY
PINK - INVESTIGATIONS

App [initials]

Man stabs brother in pork chop dispute

MILWAUKEE COUNTY MEDICAL EXAMINER

CASE NO. ...1339....

SUPPLEMENTARY

Name
Date Death 7/13/80

Sunday, 7/13/80, 10:25pm, Capt. Gorlewski, Milwaukee Police Detective Bureau, called and reported to the undersigned that a stabbing had been accomplished at ███ North 22nd Street which had resulted in the death of one person. He requested an investigator from this office respond to the scene.

Medical Examiner's Ambulance to the scene at 10:27pm.

The undersigned drove to the scene, ███ North 22nd Street, and found it to be a single family two story residence, neat, clean, and orderly.

At the scene the undersigned was met by Det. Lt. Brandt, Squad 164; Ptm. Campbell and Halverson, Squad 70 early; Ptm. James Butler, Squad 297 (photos); and Det. Schulte and Henner, Squad 105 early.

They directed the undersigned to the frontroom where the body of the deceased was seen laying in a supine position, head to the west and feet to the east. The body was lifeless and was without vital signs; obviously dead. The body had been covered with a cloth sheet on the undersigned's arrival which was removed to make a cursory examination. The deceased was fully clothed with a moderate amount of blood seen to the sport shirt. The shirt had been cut away to reveal the chest and EKG pads were afixed to the chest. A penetrating wound is seen to the left chest at the nipple level which is approximately 1" in width and ¼" in height. No blood is seen to exude from the wound.

Also present at the residence were numerous relatives. The officers present related the following account of the incident.

The house is occupied by Mr. Albert ███ Sr. 10/18/10, his wife, Rosie ███, 10/18/24, CURTIS LEE ███ N/M, 1/13/58, and others. Present this evening were the parents, Curtis, Rosemary ███ (sister), Barbara ███ (sister), and the deceased, identified as ANDREW LEE ███, age 26, born 2/14/54, address unknown, now divorced.

The deceased was in the kitchen cooking pork chops. Curtis ███ entered the kitchen and began arguing about the amount of smoke being produced by the cooking chops. They began striking each other with their fists. One of the sisters stated that Curtis picked up a butcher knife off the kitchen table and stabbed the deceased once in the chest. The deceased then fled from the kitchen, stopping in the dinning room, where he stated to his father; "Look what he done done to me." He then walked a few feet to the frontroom where he collapsed to the floor. Curtis then fled from the house taking the knife with him.

Officers responded to the scene as did the paramedics. They attached leads to the chest, found him without vital signs, and left. Other officers responding to the scene apprehended Curtis in the area. He directed the officers to a sewer grate where he stated he had thrown the knife. The officers are said to be in the process of recovering the knife at this time.

The medical examiner's ambulance arrived, they removed the body from the house, and the undersigned locked the door to the ambulance.

At the morgue P.O.David Gorecki, BofI, took 4 black and white photos of the deceased.

J.R.Endrizzi

Teen electrocuted while watching TV in tub

MILWAUKEE COUNTY MEDICAL EXAMINER

CASE NO. 177

SUPPLEMENTARY

Name RONALD [redacted]
Date Death 1/20/79

Saturday, 1/20/79, 7:28pm, Sgt. Kantor, Milwaukee Police District #4, called and stated that the body of a 15 years old white male had been found at his residence, [redacted] North 42nd Street. He stated that the body was obviously dead and that it appeared that the body had entered a bathtub at that location with an operating TV set. He stated that the matter was under investigation by Squad 49. A detective team will be sent to the scene and he requested an investigator from this office be dispatched as well. The circumstances are not completely known to him at this time.
Medical Examiner's Ambulance and Investigator Kortsch to the scene at 7:35pm.

J.R.Endrizzi

8:00 PM - Saturday - January 20, 1979 - The undersighed went to the residence and met there with Detectives R. KOWALCZYK and H.MAYER, Squad #105.
The house is an old frame structure converted into a duplex. The first floor consists of a living room which has been combined with what was originally a dining room to make one large room, two bedrooms and a bathroom.
The officers directed the attention of the undersigned to the bathroom which is located in the mid south portion of the first floor.
Against the south wall there is a white enameled bathtub standard type, 5' long by 2' high.
In the tub is the body of an adolescent white male. The body is in a seated position in the southwest corner of the tub. The head rests against the south wall near its juncture with the west wall. The legs are bent at the knee with the feet pointing to the east. The body is warm and rigid throughout. There are apparent burns to the left upper shoulder, the left armpit, the left arm and left upper chest, the left lateral upper leg and a small burn to the right upper back. The body is nude.
The tub contains water to a depth of 4". The left arm rests across the faucets on the west end of the tub. Theleft hand rests on the tub rim. The right hand rests on the top of a 12" portable Zenith television set which rests on the lap of the decedent. There is a makeshift aerial consisting of a wire clotheshanger which projects into the water from the right side of the set. The right lower portion of the set is in the water. Beneath the left buttock of the body is a slip joint pliers. On the floor in front of the tub are blue jeans and white jockey shorts. Beneath the washbowl against the west wall is a portable Realistic stereo-radio-tapeplayer AC-Battery with the plug and cord lying on the floor. The cord to the TV set rests across the washbowl with the plug in the basin. Above the washbowl is a mirrored cabinet on either side of which are fluorescent lights. On each side of the lights are electrical outlet connections.
The TV set shows the On-Off switch to be in the On position.
The plastic devices covering the VHF and UHF channel selectors are missing with the switches open and exposed to view.
Eight photographs of the scene were taken by PO BUTLER.
Onephotograph of the scene was taken by the undersigned.
The rectal temperature of the deceased is 96°.
Present at this time is ROBERT [redacted] 12-3-60, single.
He said the deceased is his brother, RONALD [redacted] born 6-2-63, single, a drop-out from Edison Junior High School, unemployed.
The other occupants of the home are their mother, MARY LOU [redacted] 9-11-29, and their step-father, RICHARD [redacted] 1-26-25.

3420

(OVER)

Also living in the flat is the girl-friend of the informant, ROBERT MYER, one NANCY ██████, born 4-21-59.
Deceased's mother and step-father left this past Thursday to go snowmobiling near Wausau, Wis.
The informant has made them aware of the death and they are returning to this city tonight.
The informant last saw deceased at 8:00 this AM when subject was watching TV on the console TV set in the living room.
Deceased seemed normal at the time.
At 8:00 AM the informant went to the basement where he has his bedroom and he said he went to sleep.
At 9:00 this AM his girl friend, NANCY ██████ returned from a neighboring bank where she had transacted some business.
She said that the Realistic stereo-radio combination portable was on and playing in the living room. She assumed deceased was in his bedroom in the southeast corner of the flat but she did not actually see or hear him at that time.
She then went downstairs where she joined ROBERT ████ in his bedroom. They said they spent the day in bed sleeping.
At about 6:45 they awoke. ROBERT ████ noticed the light in the bathroom was on but the door was locked and he obtained no response from within. He forced the lock on the door and entered to find deceased as herein previously described. The cord to the TV set was plugged into the electrical outlet on the south side of the wall cabinet. He pulled the plug from the outlet and called District #4. Para Med #4 responded also.
He said the deceased was not in poor physical or mental health.
He said decedent had never been institutionalized, was not suicidal and made no threats to do away with himself.
He said subject had some problems dealing with difficulty in adjusting to school and also had some bad experiences with the law.
A later check showed subject was arrested for rape on 10-7-78 and for burglary and loitering on 5-27-76.
He said that the portable TV set found in the tub was normally kept in deceased's bedroom. The plastic covers to the channel selector switches had broken off and deceased used a pliers to manipulate the switches to select the channels. The pliers found in the tub is the tool deceased used to manipulate the switches.
Deceased occasionally used marijuana but was not addicted to hard drugs.
The informant ROBERT ████ does not believe deceased took his own life.
The above information was relayed to Mr. WARREN B. HILL of this office who asks that the mother and step-father of the decedent be interviewed when they are available on return to this area.
The TV set and pliers were brought to this office by the undersigned.

J.Kortsch

Saturday, January 20, 1979; PO Dennis Monfre of the B of I, came to this office and took 3 photos and one identifying right index finger print on RONALD ████ B of I file #150367.

C. Borchardt

Sunday, January 21, 1979; 4:45PM, Contacted Mrs. ██████, mother of RONALD ██████. She said that she last spoke with deceased this past Thursday when she left for up north. Deceased was in good spirits and good health. He has never been depressed, not under care of any doctor or taking any medication. Deceased was warned not to plug in any appliance while taking a bath. The brother, Robert ████, mentioned that deceased would frequently take the TV into the bath tub with him while informant was out of town for the week end. He also did the same with the radio. Deceased was not attending school nor was he employed.

C. Borchardt

Lovers overcome by van fumes

MILWAUKEE COUNTY MEDICAL EXAMINER

CASE NO. 2430

SUPPLEMENTARY

Name DONALD J. ████

Date Death 12/26/80

Friday, 12/26/80, 11:25pm, Sgt. Ellis, Milwaukee Police District #2, called and reported to the undersigned that officers from his district were at 715 East ████, where, in a van parked in front of that address, the bodys of two persons had been found. They are obviously dead and have not been conveyed from the scene. He requested an investigator and ambulance respond to the location. Medical examiner's ambulance dispatched and the undersigned to scene.

At the location, a quiet residential street, the undersigned was met by Squad 2 early, Segerant Robert Surdyk, Squad 27 early, Ptm. Kraft, Squad 26 early, Ptm. Mazurek and Kubacki, and Detective Billy Harker, Squad 112 early.

The officers directed the undersigned to the van in question, a 1973 Dodge, brown in color, windows all around which are, except for the windshield and front door windows, covered with a silver plastic which permits one to see out but not see in. The license is Wisconsin 1981 auto plate SF ████, the plates listing to a station wagon belonging to a Robert M. ████, 2573 South ████, not to the vehilce on which the plates are found.

In the van, when the rear doors are opened, are the bodies of the decedents; SANDRA A. ████, white female, 12/27/64, of ████ South 23rd Street, and DONALD J. ████, white male, 8/23/64, of W182 S6521 ████ Drive, Muskego. This identification is from ID papers found in the vehicle and not from actual identification of the subjects by persons present or knowing them.

The bodies are situated in the rear compartment of the vehicle behind the rear seats in a large open, flat area which is covered with blue pile carpeting set loosely on the floor. Both of the victims are prone, heads towards the front of the vehicle. The female is clad in a black sweater. Her overalls are pulled down as are her panties and are about her left ankle. Her arms are flexed at the elbows her right arm being under the male's torso. She is positione so that she is parallel with the left inside wall of the van, approximately 1 foot from the left wall.

The male is clad in a brown plaid shirt, cotton flannel, and is also in a prone position, thought slightly on his left side. He is somewhat diagonal to the female and much more to the front of the open carpeted area. His head is partially under the rear seat, his torso being on top of the females left arm and his legs being almost to the right inner wall of the van. In addition to the shirt the decedent has a pair of blue jeans on and pulled down about his ankles. He is clad in jockey type shorts, white in color, which are up, covering his buttocks. When the bodies were removed from the van a plaid 3/4 length coat was found under the bodies as was a dinner plate, which was found between the heads of the decedents. The plate was clean and had a patterned border. On top of the rear bench type seat was found a red suede waist length jacket consistant with the females size, a nylon purse with the female's identification, and a black leather waist length jacket consistant with the male's size. Between the front seats is a capped bottle of CHELLA LAMBRUSCO wine which is approximately 3/4 full. It is the 1.75 liter bottle. The bottle is in a brown paper bag and contains a receipt listing the purchase date as 12/26/80 No name is found on the receipt. Also found in the front seat area is a glass which has no residue or liquid and an unopened 12oz can of PEPSI COLA.

The officers gave the following information.

This date at approximately 8:30pm, Ptm. Kraft was sent to the scene on a citizen's complaint of a "van running unattended." The officer was questioned by the undersigned and stated that he had arrived and found the van running, all doors locked. He looked inside the vehicle as well as he could and could see no one inside. He shined his flashlight inside and attempted to open the van to look inside. He could not enter. At this point he went to several of the neighboring homes including the complainant's home, 715 East ████. None of the neighbors knew sho the van belonged to and it was at that point that the officer issued a parking ticket to the van for operation of a vehicle while unattended. The undersigned later closed all the doors to the vehicle and used a flashlight to look inside, same conditions encountered by the original officer on the scene; the bodies still inside the vehicle. The undersigned

(continued)

continued

was unable to see clearly what was inside and could not, from the front of the vehicle see the bodies. As the undersigned knew what he was looking for the general shapes and outlines could barely be discerned. In the undersigned's opinion, it is understandable how the officer could have failed to notice the bodies in the van.

At 10:35pm, the complainant at 715 East ██████ called for the police again and Squad 26 early responded to the scene. It was at that time that the officers forced the driver's wing window and entered, finding the bodies of the decedents.

The undersigned then interviewed the complainant; Mrs. Eileen R. ██████, W/F, 4/2/27, 715 East ██████, 481█████. She stated that this evening her daughter, Karen, 11/25/52, was at home and her boyfriend came over to visit her. The boyfriend, Ronald ██████, 10/8/51, of 7239 North ██████, Glendale, spoke with the complainant and Mrs. ██████ stated that that the van outside had been bothering her; the muffler was quite loud. The boyfriend then went out and pounded on the windows, he received no response. He looked in the windows and saw no one. A passerby was stopped by him and asked by Herte if the van was his. The passerby, name unknown, stood at the window and looked in. He stated to Herte that someone inside looked up at him and waved. ██████ then went back inside and the passerby walked on. This took place at about 6:15pm.

By 8:15pm she was more disturbed and called the police. She observed the officer arrive, pound on the windows, try the doors, and shine his flashlight inside the van. The officer then came to her home and talked with her. He also went to several of the neighbors and spoke with them. She observed him write the ticket and leave.

By 10:15pm she was even more disturbed and called the police again. The police arrived shortly thereafter and broke into the van. She does not know the names of the victims, does not know the van, and has not seen it in the area before.

The bodies were removed from the van by R&R Conveyers, the doors to the ambulance being locked at the scene by the undersigned. All personal property except the wine was removed in the ambulance with the bodies. The wine was taken into evidence by Detective Hacker.

Detective Hacker stated he would go with a late shift detective to the ██████ home to make notification. The undersigned requested that the parents or someone else be directed to come to the medical examiner's office to make identification. They stated this would be done.

J.R.Endrizzi

Friday, 12/26/80, 11:25pm, At the scene the undersigned examined the van in question.

The exhaust system on the van is defective. There is a hole in the muffler, which is rested. The exhaust pipe extends from the rear of the muffler to the rear of the vehicle. It is obviously intended to extend back to the left rear wheel housing, pass over the rear axle, and to the rear of the vehicle. The exhaust pipe is well rusted and extends up over the rear left axle, where it is rusted off. The exhaust issues into the left rear wheel housing, fills same, and then billows from the wheel housing and the back of the vehicle. The gas tank is almost empty and the keys were in the ignition when found. The van was running as noted earlier in the report. The interior of the vehicle was filled with exhaust fumes and was very warm according to the first officers to see the victims.

J.R.Endrizzi

Saturday December 27,1980;2:00AM

Deputy JAMES ██████ came to the County Morgue and identified DONALD ██████ as the boyfriend of Sandra Urbanski (Case # 2430). The family was then notified of the death by Deputy ██████.

Thomas F. Hanratty

Harassed school teacher kills wife, 90, and self, 59

MILWAUKEE COUNTY MEDICAL EXAMINER

CASE NO. 861

SUPPLEMENTARY

Name Frank █████
Date Death April 27,81

Monday April 27,81 9:15AM PO Hawkins, Oak Creek Police Department called this office and stated that two bodies had been found at █████ S. Wayland Dr. The officer requested an investigator from this office be dispatched to the scene.

9:35AM The undersigned proceeded to █████ S. Wayland Dr. and was met by Capt. Prochnow and Det. Look of the Oak Creek Police Department along with severeal uniform officers. The officers stated that they were called this morning by Rev. Johnson of the Oak Creek Community Church. Rev. Johnson requested the officers check on the welfare of the residents at the above address as they had not been at services on 4/26/81 and were known to have family problems. At 9:00AM Sgt. Stahl responded to the call. Upon his arrival the Sgt. found the residence closed but unlocked. Entering the front door the officer called out to no avail. Further inspection of the residence revealed the bodies identified as Frank █████, DOB 8/30/21 and Octavia █████, DOB 2/7/91 in the rear bedroom.

The undersigned was directed inside the residence which is a single family dwelling located on the west side of Waylnad Dr. Upon entering the residence a person can turn right into the livingroom or proceeded straight through a short hallway into the kitchen. On the kitchen table is a letter which is undated which reads; Send our bodies to this funeral home. They have info as to where we are to be buried. Caskets to be closed & only a private funeral. Mr. & Mrs. F █████ Call Raymond Urban- on the bottom of the letter are a business card for Raymond L. Urban, Attorney at Law and a match book from the Kutis Funeral Home, Affton Mo. Next to the letter are the subject's wallets which contain identification belonging to Octavia █████ and Frank █████. Both wallets are intact and contain sums of money. The undersigned was than directed to the bedroom located in the northwest corner of the house. Entering the room the body identified as Frank █████, age 59 can be seen directly in front of the door. The subject is in a supine position with his head to the north and fett to the south. The lower legs and feet are crossed giving the impression that the subject rolled over or twisted as he collapsed. The subject is fully dressed in a T shirt, trousers and socks. There are 3 circular perforations to the mid anterior torso of the shirt. The subject has dried blood about the anterior torso and right hand. About 3' west of Frank █████ is the body identified as his wife Octavia Veres, DOB 2/7/91. Mrs. █████'s body is in a supine position on the single bed with her head to the south and feet to the north. The subject is dressed in a house dress and stockings. To the mid anterior torso just inferior of the sternum are 3 circular perforations. There is dried blood about the area of the wounds. The body appears undisturbed with her eyeglasses in place and a towel covering the face but not wrapped about the head. A further search of the room revaled an empty .22 cal. casing on the bed on the left side of Mrs. █████. Under the bed are two empty .22 cal. casings along with what appears to be a spent .22 cal. missile. To the right side of the body of Mr. █████ is a spent .22 cal. casing as well as one to the left side of the torso. Under a chair along the south wall near Mr. █████'s feet is a spent .22 Cal Casing. On the floor just above Mr. █████'s head is a spent .22 cal. missile which is intact not showing any signs of distortion. Near Mr. █████'s right hand is a .22 cal. automatic, Sturm Ruger, serial number 13-78927. No model number is listed. A check of the weapon reveals one live .22 cal. long rifle in the chamber however the clip is empty. A further search of the room reveals a slight amount of dried blood on the carpet between the body of Mr. █████ and the bed on which he wife lays. A further search of the residence reveals it to be very neat and clean with no signs of foul play.

OVER

Mr. Raymond Urban, Attorney arrived at the residence and produced copies of the wills for Frank and Octavia ████ which directs him to be their personal representative. Mr. Urban stated that for some time the subject has been depressed over the ill health of his aging wife and the conditions at work. The subject was a teacher at Audubon Middle Jr. High and since the desegregation he has been unable to teach or control the children. Mr. Urban stated that the subject also had trouble with children in the neighborhood often reporting them to the police for various activity. Mr. Urban stated that the subject came to his office on 4/16/81 at which time he gave him the key to the residence in case something happened. Mr. ████ also gave the informant the name of Mary ████, 1241 ████ St. apt. #631, Bridgeport Conn. as the person to notify in case of emergency. During the conversation the subject indicated that was had about 50 sick days which he could take prior to his retirement at the end of the year. Mr. Urban looked at the note found on the kitchen table and identified the handwriting as that of Mr. ████. Mr. Urban also stated that on 4/17/81 the subject called him sounding very depressed. The informant along with the Oak Creek Police Department came to the residence. During this conversation the subject indicated his intent to do away with himself and his wife. The officers took a shotgun from the home after Rev. Johnson arrived and spoke with the subject. This was confirmed by the officers. A further search of the residence revealed a note in the mailbox indicating that the mail was removed from the box because it had not been picked up for four days. The note was dated 4/27/81. Also in the livingroom of the residence was the TV Screen which was opened and folded to the programing for 4/22/81. Nothing further could be detected at the scene relevant to the death. The bodies were removed via Medical Examiner's Ambulance. The residence was left in the custody of Mr. Urban with nothing further being removed.

The undersigned contact Audubon Middle Jr. High School and spoke with Mr. Hatton. The informant stated that Mr. ████ was employed as a teacher. Mr. Hatton stated that he was aware of the subject having some problems. The informant stated that he was off last week however he was given a letter this morning, from Mr. ████ dated 4/21/81 requesting a leave of absence. The person who received the letter is on vacation this week however she left a note that she attempted to contact the subject via phone to no avail.

R. Goeb

Monday May 4,81 10:00AM Dr. Darien returned a call to this office regarding Octavia and Frank ████. The doctor stated that both people had been under his care since 1967. Mr. ████ was not being treated for any chronic conditions just routine checkups. Mrs. ████ did have some heart failure and hypertension however this was very well controlled and for a person of 90 years was able to get about very well. Mr. and Mrs. ████ came to the office on 4/21/81 at which time Mr. ████ claimed that he was very nervous and upset over his wife's condition wanting to stay home to care for her. The doctor wrote a letter asking Mr. ████ be given a medical leave of absence to accomplish this. The doctor stated that a no time did he detect any signs of depression.

R. Goeb

Coin dealer hangs self in auto-erotic misadventure

MILWAUKEE COUNTY MEDICAL EXAMINER

CASE NO. 1144

SUPPLEMENTARY

Name KEITH [redacted]
Date Death 6/7/78

Wednesday, 6/7/78, 9:45pm, Dispatcher Morris, Glendale Police Department, called and stated that officers from his department were at [redacted] West Silver Spring Drive, a business complex, where the body of an adult white male had been found. He requested an investigator and ambulance be dispatched to the scene.

The undersigned drove to the scene and later, at 10:05pm, requested the ambulance.

The undersigned was met at the scene by Glendale Police Officers Ziebell and Malloy, Sqd. 1706, and Detective Porth. Also at the scene were Sherry [redacted], W/F, 10/21/48, of [redacted] North 100th Street, Apt. #108, and Roy [redacted], W/M, 8/3/1897, of [redacted] North 36th Street.

The officers directed the undersigned to the offices of Numismatic Investments Inc. and through the showroom into a back room work area. There the body of the deceased, KEITH [redacted], white male, 27 years of age, born 10/4/50, of [redacted] North 100th Street, Apt. #108, was seen. The body was in a supine position with the head and neck being elevated. There is a length of heavy brown rough textured rope about the neck and strung up to a length of conduit and then over and about a 2 X 8 rafter. The body is cool and limp and is obviously dead. It rests on a slanted board which is covered with a smooth heavy cloth of golden color. The board is approximately 5 feet in length and 3 feet in width and is of ½" thickness. To the north of the body is an open July issue of Playboy magazine which is turned to the three page centerfold. Found to the east of the body, near the feet, was a plastic bottle of dermesage lotion. The body is nude with the clothing piled neatly to the north of the body. Numerous boxes, cases, and folders of coins are near the body and later it was determined by an employee that nothing had been disturbed.

The undersigned then interviewed Ms. [redacted]. She stated that she had been dating the deceased for the past three years. Approximately 3 years ago they opened a coin shop at the Bay-Shore Shopping Center. They operated the shop with the deceased acting as president of the firm and the informant acting as vice-president until approximately one year ago at which time they moved to their present location. She stated that they continued as partners and the business was going well. The deceased was not in financial difficulties, had no medical problems, and was not depressed. She stated that she knew of no threats against the deceased, no robberies, attempt robberies, burglaries, or attempt burglaries, nor any other criminal activities in which the deceased might have been a victim or participant. She stated that approximately 6 months ago the deceased saw a Playboy magazine on the cover of which was a female standing with her legs spread wide apart, masterbating, with a rope about her neck. He stated to her that this; "really turns me on." He repeatedly mentioned the picture to her and asked her several times to bind him and perform sexual acts with her. She stated that she and the deceased had been engaging in regular sexual activity for some time; however, she refused to engage in the bondage. She stated that the deceased moved in with her in February 1978, she being divorced, her husband already being remarried. She stated that there was no animosity between her ex-husband and the deceased.

She stated that she last saw the deceased alive at 9:45am this date when he left for work. She called and spoke with by phone at 4:00pm and he stated that he was bored, the day had been slow. He stated he had had one good sale, that being for approximately $500.00 worth of silver dollars. She stated that she was preparring barbequed ribs for dinner and he stated he would be home at 6:00pm. When he did not arrive she called the shop and received no answer. She then drove to several locations after checking the shop and seeing it dark. She then returned to the shop and entered. She found the deceased as noted and called for the police. She stated that she and the deceased were the only persons with keys to the premises and later added that the owner of the building also had a key.

Following the body examination at the scene and removal

3420

(OVER)

by the medical examiner's ambulance, it's doors being locked by the undersigned, the undersigned examined the board on which the deceased had been laying. [redacted] stated that it was at the store when they moved in and the deceased used it to sort coins. She stated that it had been in a storage area earlier in the day. She was questioned again about possible financial problems and stated that a civil suit against the deceased had been settled against the deceased in February 1978 in the amount of $140,000.00 which was expected to be appealed by the deceased. She stated that this had no been bothering the deceased.

The undersigned then examined the area where the deceased was found and examined the rope and the manner in which it was attached. Prior to the removal of the body the undersigned had measured the distance from the conduit, where the rope passed over it, to the deceased's neck and found it to be exactly 72". The board appears to have been proped at an angle of approximately 45° resting one end on a shelf and the other end on the floor. It would appear that the deceased entered the room, positioned the board, removed his clothing, positioned the rope about his neck after first placing the end over the 2by8 rafter one time, looping the rope over itself, and then running the rope over a piecte of conduit and down to the top of the board. He then applied the dermassage cream to his penis and permitted himself to slide down the board thereby creating tension on the rope. The entire apparatus gives the impression of having been constructed to achieve autoerrotic ends.

The undersigned then removed the rope from the scene, a signed property receipt being received by the undersigned.

Upon returning to the office the undersigned received a call from a local reporter inquiring about the case. He related the following; In 1971 the deceased and another man were arrested by officers of the U.S.Secret Service and Postal Inspectors for fraudently altering coins. In 1973, according to the informant, he was convicted and sentenced to 5 years probation by Judge Myron Gordon. What,if any, bearing to the death of the deceased may exist to these facts is unknown at present.

James R. Endrizzi

Boy slays playmate with "empty rifle"

MILWAUKEE COUNTY MEDICAL EXAMINER

CASE NO. 2 1 4 7

SUPPLEMENTARY

Name MARK ████

Date Death November 9,1978

Thursday November 9, 1978; 2:10AM

E. MEHL, RN, the night supervisor of nursing at St. Luke's Hospital, called to report the death in surgery of MARK ████, 14 years old, DOB 1/1/1964, of ████ South 50th Street (546████). According to the informant, the subject was brought to the hospital from an unknown location by the Greenfield Fire Department, admitted on 11/8/78 at 7:00PM with a gunshot wound to the chest. The subject was unconscious on admission and taken to surgery where DR. JAMES AUER operated until 12:30AM, at which time the death pronouncement was made. A bullet was recovered from the subject's clothing and is presently in the Pathology Department. It will be held until this office or the Police pick it up. The body will be held until this office makes the removal from the hospital.

Spoke briefly with Mrs. DARLENE ████, the mother of the deceased. She stated that the deceased was shot by his best friend, accidently, at the friend's home. Mrs. ████ was concerned with the necessity for an autopsy on her son, but , after some conversation, said that she realized the necessity for it.

Medical Examiner's Ambulance dispatched to the hospital.

Thomas F. Hanratty T. F. H.

Thursday November 9, 1978; 2:50AM

Sgt. JAMES SCHEIDT, Greenfield Police Department, returned a call from this office. He said that the reports concerning the shooting of MARK W.████ are on tape and will be typed up later. A copy of the report will be dispatched to this office as soon as it becomes available. A summary by Detective JOHN HICKMAN is as follows:

ROY R.████, 12 years old, DOB 4/24/1966, of 4537 West ████ Avenue (321████), spent yesterday afternoon cleaning his .22 caliber Mauser semi-automatic rifle, in preparation for hunting. He filled the cartridge tube beneath the barrel with 15 .22 rounds to see how many shells the weapon held. He then emptied the tube and shook the rifle. Hearing no rattle, Roy assummed that the weapon was empty. He told the officer that he doesn't remember pulling back the slide to put a round into the chamber. At about 5:30PM to 5:45PM, his friend MARK ████ came to the house and the boys went into the bedroom where the "unloaded" rifle lay on the bed. Roy said that he was "just goofing around" when he picked up the rifle , pointed it at Mark and pulled the trigger. The rifle discharged and Mark fell forward, clutching his chest.

The Sergerant will dispatch an officer to the hospital to pick up the bullet.

Thomas F. Hanratty T. F. H.

11/9/78 9:10 AM GLORIA RIEGERT, medical records supervisor at St. Luke's Hospital, returned a call from the undersigned and stated that, while hospitalized, MARL W.████ received twelve units of whole blood, two units of fresh frozen plasma, and two units of platelet concentrate. She states that she is checking on the toxicology record and the medication record, and that when they become available she will call back.

Robert E. Schultz R. E. S.

3420

(over)

11/9/78 9:30 AM GLORIA RIEGERT, above, called back and stated that the only tests recorded for MARK W. [redacted] were routine blood tests, count, typing, gasses, etc., with no toxicological evaluations. She states that the record does not indicate the administration of any medications.

Robert E. Schultz R.E.S.

11/9/78, 9:25 A. M.: The undersigned proceeded to 4537 West [redacted] Avenue, Greenfield, WI. Interviewed was ROY ARTHUR [redacted], white male, age: 12, date of birth: 4-24-66, attending Greenfield Middle School, presently in 7th Grade. He related that on November 8, 1978, he was in his bedroom and had taken a .22 caliber rifle, which was his father's gun and which had been stored under his bed for five years, for the purpose of cleaning same as they were intent on going squirrel hunting. He related that he and the deceased, MARK W. [redacted], and his brother, ROBB, and his father have, on occasions, gone squirrel hunting together. Upon removing the rifle from beneath the bed, he proceeded to clean it; and after cleaning it, proceeded to load the cartridge tube beneath the barrel and was able to insert fifteen .22 caliber shells. He does not remember using the bolt action to place one of the shells in the chamber. After inserting the fifteen shells, he then proceeded to unload the gun, shaking it out upon his bed. He did not count the shells as they fell from the weapon. He then took the shells and placed them in the box, put the shells into the ammunition box, and put that box on the coffee table in the living room. This was about 5:10 P. M. as his mother then called him to eat supper. He then went into the kitchen, sat down and had his supper; and about 5:30 - 5:40 P. M., his brother, ROBB, age: 16, date of birth: 4-18-62, came into the hallway with MARK [redacted]. Mark stood in the hallway for a few minutes, and then he and MARK entered his bedroom. MARK noticed the gun on the bed, and "I picked it up and told him it held fifteen shells; and then just goofing around, I pointed the rifle at MARK and pulled the trigger. The gun went off, and MARK had a funny look on his face and said, 'I've been shot,' - and with that, he grasped his chest. We just stood there and looked at one another in shock, and my parents came running into the bedroom. MARK started to fall to the floor, and we grabbed him and helped him onto the floor. He then said, 'My God, I am paralyzed.'" With that MR. [redacted] ran to the telephone and summoned the GREENFIELD POLICE AND RESCUE SQUAD. Prior to the Rescue Squad's arrival, his parents removed a wad of chewing gum from MARK's mouth. When the Rescue Squad arrived, they attempted resuscitation, but to no avail. They then conveyed MARK to the hospital. He appeared to be dead at the time they took him out of the house. Informant then related that, after he shot MARK with the rifle, he threw it upon the bed, and that is where the GREENFIELD police found the weapon, and they presently have the weapon and the ammunition on inventory. Informant further stated that he never, at any time, had any arguments with MARK and had been his friend for the past two years, and they attended the same school. Further, that, on their hunting trips in the past, he and MARK had both used other weapons belonging to the family to hunt squirrels. During the interview with the informant, the undersigned noted that the informant was apparently still in shock, crying profusely; and with great difficulty, he related the incident.

Also interviewed at the scene were the mother, HELEN [redacted], and her son, ROBB, age: 16. Both of them related the circumstances as stated by the informant, ROY [redacted]. It is the opinion of the undersigned that this incident was purely an accidental incident. There did not appear to be anything suspicious at the time of the interview.

James J. Behrendt (slb) JJB

COUNTY OF LOS ANGELES
DEPARTMENT OF CHIEF MEDICAL EXAMINER – CORONER
MEDICAL REPORT

Name: JANIS JOPLIN

Case No. 70–10463

Date: 10-4-70

Dr. ______

CONTINUATION SHEET

Information from Sgt. Sanchez, DHQ and John Cooke, same addr. as Decedent, Apt. 223 (851-2000), working under Contract c̄ Decedent's group:

Decedent was 27-year-old, female, and stage singer by occupation. Her group is called "Joplin Full Tilt Boogie" composed of herself and group of musicians – under "Fantality Inc." licensed to engage in the State of California. On 10-3-70 at about 2400 hrs., Decedent was in studio at "Sunset Sound Recorder" located on Sunset. After recording some music, Decedent together c̄ another man (unknown name & addr.) dropped in at "Barney's Beanery" at 8447 Sta. Monica Blvd. and took about two drinks. Decedent was last seen alive by Jack Hagyo, mgr. of Apartment (851-2000) about 0100 hrs., 10-4-70, coming home, alone.

This evening, before 1915 hrs., Mr. Cooke, (alone) saw Decedent's car outside of the garage. Concerned why the car was parked outside, Cooke called up Decedent between 1915 – 1950 hrs. 10-4-70, but no response. He then borrowed key of the manager, entered the room and found Decedent lying on the floor between chair and bed, appr. dead. Cooke then called Decedent's lawyer & a doctor and called police. R-A. #35 at scene 2110 hrs. 10-4-70 and pronounced death same hour.

Decedent was obs. lying on her left side, clad c̄ blouse and panties. No rigor mortis noted and livor mortis about 4+. A small laceration on the lower lip of Decedent noted poss. due to fall. Multiple needle marks (fresh) noted on the left antecubital fossa and old marks on the right. The airconditioner at scene was on & no signs of struggle noted in the room. Dalmane capsules and tablets for pain found on bed.

No signs of trauma or foul play.

F. Loza
Ch

76M118U – 3/70

COUNTY OF LOS ANGELES

DEPARTMENT OF CHIEF MEDICAL EXAMINER - CORONER

MEDICAL REPORT

Name: Janis Joplin

Case No. 70-10463

Date: 10-5-70

Dr. ____________

CONTINUATION SHEET

1100 hrs - Arrived at decedent's residence (7047 Franklin Avenue, Apt. 105) with Dr. Noguchi, Dr. Katsuyama and William Lystrup for further investigation. Public Administrator seal broken and apartment entered by above.

1110 hrs - Gauze noted on decedent's bed; gauze found in waste basket in livingroom with apparent dried blood residue.

1120 hrs - The end of a red balloon or rubber glove was found in a waste basket in decedent's kitchen containing a white powder. A large disposable towel was found with apparent dried blood residue with below evidence.

1140 hrs - An apparent hype kit consisting of a teaspoon with black smudge, a small piece of cotton and dried residue; a needle and plastic syringe containing a clear liquid and a paper package containing a brownish white powder was found in the top right dresser drawer in decedent's livingroom. Also found in the drawer was a plastic bag containing possible marijuana, and a small plastic bag with 4-1/2 small white tablets "Lilly 172."

1200 hrs - All above evidence was impounded and brought in and decedent's residence was locked and re-sealed by the undersigned.

C. R. Dambacher

C R Dambacher

76M118U - 3/70

Janis Joplin

Information from Sgt. Sanchez and John Coake, same address as the decedent, apartment 223, working under contract with decedent's (music) group:

Decedent was 27-year-old female and stage singer by occupation. Her group is called "Joplin Full Tilt Boogie" composed of herself and group of musicians - under "Fantality Inc." licensed to engage in the State of California.

On 10-3-70 at about 2400 hours (midnight), decedent was in studio at "Sunset Sound Recorder" located on Sunset Blvd. After recording some music, decedent together with another man (unknown name and address) dropped in at "Barney's Beanery" at 8447 Santa Monica Blvd. and took about two drinks. Decedent was last seen alive by Jack Hagyo, manager of apartment, about 0100 hours, (1 a.m.), 10-4-70, coming home, alone.

This evening, before 1915 hours (7:15 p.m.), Mr. Cooke saw decedent's car outside of the garage. Concerned why the car was parked outside, Cooke called up the decedent between 1915-1950 hours, (7:15-7:50 p.m.), 10-4-70, but no response. He then borrowed key of the manager, entered the room and found decedent lying on the floor between chair and bed, apparently dead. Cooke then called decedent's lawyer and a doctor and called police. R.A. No. 35 at scene 2110 hours (9:10 p.m.), 10-4-70 and pronounced death same hour.

Decedent was observed lying on her left side, clad with blouse and panties. No rigor mortis noted and (not readable) mortis about four times. A small laceration on the lower lip of decedent noted, possibly due to fall. Multiple needle marks (fresh) noted on the left (not readable) and odd marks on the right. The air conditioner at scene was on and no signs of struggle noted in the room. Dalmane capsules and tablets for pain found on bed. No signs of trauma or foul play.

Army colonel falls to death after martini binge

MILWAUKEE COUNTY MEDICAL EXAMINER

CASE NO. 2166

SUPPLEMENTARY

Name JAMES E. ████████
Date Death November 21,1979

Wednesday November 21, 1979; 11:50PM

DR. KASTENSEN called from Milwaukee County General Hospital to report the death of an Unidentified White Male, age about 40 years old, brought to the hospital from 758 North Broadway, the Milwaukee Athletic Club, undressed on admission, cool and limp with a possible neck fracture. The subject was bleeding from both ears and his ribs were fractured. The deceased had fallen from a 3rd story window, or from some other high structure at the Club. The Dead On Arrival pronouncement was made at 10:50PM.

11/21/1979; 11:55PM

Detectives GUY and BECKER, Squad # 113, Milwaukee Police Department, came to this office. They said that the deceased has been identified as one JAMES E. ████████, 48 years old, DOB 12/11/1930, single, of ████ West Willow Court, Apartment # 246 (351████). The subject was a Colonel in the Army Reserve stationed in Milwaukee. At about 6:00PM, the deceased arrived at the bar in the Milwaukee Athletic Club and during the evening with friends, consumed five or six martinis. At bout 9:00PM, the Colonel switched to Pepsi. During the evening, he met a friend, one ARTHUR P. ████████, 57 years old, of ████ North Woodward (332-████), and he was to be driven home by ████. ████ told the deceased to wait while he got his car. Colonel ████████ was to wait in the lobby, and he walked out of the bar while Brazy went to the parking lot. As ████████ arrived downstairs in the lobby, however, he found the deceased lying on the lobby floor, apparently having fallen over the three foot high railing on the third floor balcony. The night manager of the Milwaukee Athletic Club, one LOUIS ████████, 34 years old, DOB 9/7/1945, of ████ North 33rd (442████), was standing in the lobby at 10:04PM when he heard a "thud". He then noted the deceased lying on the floor of the lobby and called the Paramedics who worked on the subject, then conveyed to County Hospital. There were no witnesses found who saw the man go over the railing, or fall to the lobby floor. There is a circular marble staircase rising from the lobby, surrounded by a 3 foot railing. The bar, which is located on the third floor, leads out onto the balcony which this staircase serves. The distance fallen is either 50 or 55 feet, depending on whether the deceased had gone down one flight of stairs to the first landing before falling, or whether he had dropped from the balcony itself. The lobby itself is carpeted.

Waitresses at the Club were questioned and it was determined that the deceased arrived alone and met some friends after a short while. He did not appear despondent or depressed. The police could find nothing suspicious at the scene.

Thomas F. Hanratty TFH.

Thursday November 22,1979; 6:00AM

Contacted Milwaukee Police Sgt. BILAK who is a member of the 84th Division Army Reserve unit. He contacted a Major RONALD LAMPING who works with the deceased JAMES ████████ at the unit.

Called Major LAMPING (476████) and he stated that he will go to the Reserve Unit and look up the deceased's civilian record to determine who the next of kin may be. Major Lamping works with the deceased and stated that the deceased never married and has no living parents or siblings. However, he may have a cousin listed and that name will be turned over to this office. If no civilian record lists a next of kin, Major Lamping will attempt to check Colonel ████████'s military record, located at a different location. Major Lamping will call this office shortly.

Thomas F. Hanratty TFH

3420

Thursday, 11/22/79, 8:55 AM: Major Lamping made a return call and related that JAMES E. [redacted]'s military emergency data record list his next of kin as Mrs F. [redacted] (aunt) [redacted] S. 52nd St. West Milwaukee Police were contacted and they agreed to go to the above adress and have the aunt call this office.

Thursday, 11/22/79, 9:10 AM: Robert Means called this office and related that he was a cousin of JAMES E. [redacted]. His mother is Frances [redacted] and is the aunt of the deceased. Mrs Means is currently visiting in Madison and informant will notify her and help with the burial arangements. Informant said he did not know any medical problems concerning deceased but said about a year ago deceased had been in the hospital with an unknown problem. He said the hospital was down by the lake front.

John J. Guss JJG

Thursday, November 22, 1979: Contacted St. Mary's, Columbia, Trinity Memorial and VA Hospitals in reference to any medical history on the deceased Col. James [redacted]. All hospitals advised that they had no records on the deceased being treated.

William L. Harling WLH

Thursday, 11/22/79, 9:10PM, Detective Guy of the Milwaukee Police Department called to state that he learned from Chris Seraphim that a Col Jacobs, Personnel Officer of the 84th Division, would have any further next of kin information, should this office be interested.

C. Borchardt CB

Woman stricken after grandson shot by cop

MILWAUKEE COUNTY MEDICAL EXAMINER

CASE NO. 1570

SUPPLEMENTARY

Name IRENE [redacted]
Date Death 8/22/80

Friday, 8/22/80, 8:55PM, Jean Comstock RN, called from Mt. Sinai Hospital to report that Para Tech ambulance conveyed IRENE [redacted] 65, dob 9-28-1914, from [redacted] West Highland, 344-[redacted]. Dr. Phade made DOA pronouncement at 7:50PM. Deceased is clad in a robe, body is warm and limp, no sign of trauma. Informant requested to have the funeral director call this office before release of the body.

C. Borchardt

Friday, August 22, 1980: 8:55PM: Received a call from PO HUTCHINSON, Squad # 36, reporting his investigation into a DOA death. Deceased is Irene D. [redacted], white female, age, 65, date of birth, 9-28-14; of [redacted] West Highland, Apartment # 205, phone (344-[redacted]). Informant stated that the deceased had collapsed on the street at approximately 2010 North 32nd street at which time the rescue squad was called with Med # 5 responding. Informant stated that the deceased had been worked on at the scene for approximately one hour at which time she was transported into Mount Sinai Hospital where she was pronounced DOA by Dr. PHADE at 7:52PM this date. Informant stated that the deceased was the grandmother of a Bryan [redacted] who had been shot this date by a police officer at North 32nd and Brown streets and the deceased was alledgedly at the scene. Informant stated that the deceased's daughter was the mother of [redacted] and she was presently at Milwaukee County General Hospital where the son is being operated on. Informant stated that he had notified a grandson, Jeffery [redacted], age, 19, of [redacted] North 31st Street, no phone of this death. Informant stated that additional information could be received from Det BESLEY. Informant stated that he has no medical history on the deceased.

8-22-80: 9:05PM: Contacted Detective BESLEY Squad # 161 (early) for additional information in this case. Informant stated that from information received from Detective Mike LA POINTE, Squad # 113 (early) who was present at the time was that the deceased, Irene [redacted] had come to the scene of her grandson's shooting by a police officer at North 32nd and Brown streets and had approached the grandson who had been laying at the scene prior to his removal to Milwaukee County General Hospital. Informant stated that another grandson,((name unknown at this time) had struck the deceased in the face causing her to fall backwards. Informant stated that the deceased had got up and had stated at that time " I don't feel too good" and a short time later, collapsed. Informant stated that from information received, the deceased has a history of high blood pressure and the deceased's daughter, Nancy [redacted] is presently at Milwaukee County General Hospital where her son BRYAN is being operated on at this time. Informant stated that the whole family is very hostile at this time to anyone that is a police officer and it will be very difficult to receive any additional information from the deceased's daughter. Informant stated that in addition to the grandson being operated on at the hospital, two other grandson's including Jeffery [redacted] are presently in custody for incidents at the scene. Informant was advised that the undersigned would contact Dave LIVINGSTON, Assistant Deputy Medical Examiner and advise him of the above for possible transport of the deceased into the County Morgue for autopsy.

8-22-80: 9:20PM: Contacted Dave LIVINGSTON, Assistant Deputy Medical Examiner and advised him of the above information. Informant stated that due to the deceased having collapsed just after the fall she had when struck by her grandson the body will be transported into the County Morgue.

3420

(OVER)

(Cont.)

Friday, August 22, 1980: 9:30PM: Detective BESLEY advised of the deceased being transported into the County Morgue for possible autopsy on 8-23-80.

William L. Harling WH

(*)8/23/80, 12:45 AM

Detective LaPointe, #113, called this office. He states the grandson who allegedly struck the deceased, is Timothy Michael ██████, age 23, dob-4/23/1957, of ████ North 32nd Street. The grandson denies striking the deceased.

E.Himmelreich EH

8/23/80, 7:45 AM.

Tech D.Fuhrman, B of I, came to this office and took 2 photos of the deceased.

E.Himmelreich EH

8/23/80 1:30 PM TECH. JACK R. PATTERSON of the Milwaukee Police Department Bureau of Identification came to the County Morgue and took three black and white photos and one full set of fingerprints of the deceased, IRENE ███████.

Robert E. Schultz R.E.S.

Slap on head is fatal to man

MILWAUKEE COUNTY MEDICAL EXAMINER

CASE NO. 2248

SUPPLEMENTARY

Name MICHAEL GERALD ████
Date Death 12/6/1980

December 6,1980; Saturday, 4:15 AM.

Patricia Gosch RN., St Mary's hospital, called this office to report the death of MICHAEL G. ████, age 30, dob-12/30/1949, single of 1738 North ████ Avenue, Apt. #8. The deceased had been brought to the hospital by a private auto driven by and from a place unknown to the informant. The deceased was admitted on December 2,1980 at 3:30 AM. Admission diagnosis: epidermal hematoma to right head. The deceased was conscious on admission and stated that he worked at a nursing home and he had been struck by one of the patients. The statment was questionable according to the informant. The deceased's condition deteriated and he became comatose at 5:30 AM. A right temporal crainiotomy for removal of the hematoma was performed by Dr. Suberviola. The deceased remained comatose. He expired at 4:05 this AM, 12/6/80, pronounced by Dr. Dorow. Cause of death is: complications of injury. The informant was told to but a hold on the body.

12/6/80, 4:40 AM. Medical Examiner's Ambulance (R&R conveyors) sent.

12/6/80, 5:00 AM.

Detective Lt. G.Hasting called this office and states that the deceased's mother, a patient at St Michael's Hospital has been notified of the deceased demise by Dr. Suberviola. According to Lt. Hastings, the mother questions reason for autopsy.

E.Himmelreich EH

Saturday December 6, 1980-4:20 AM - LT. HASTING, of the Milwaukee detective bureau, called this office regarding the demise of MICHAEL GERALD ████, age 30 years dob 12/30/1949, single white male of 1738 North ████ Avenue, apartment # 8.
Lt. Hasting stated, that he has a report filed by DET. W. TINGUE squad # 101 who investigated the circumstances. Det. Tingue stated, that the deceased was at Hooligans Bar, at East North Ave and North Farwell Ave. on December 1, 1980. He met a MARGORIE ████, age 26 years dob 3/29/1954 of 7341 North ████ Road and YASIN ████, age 25 years dob 9/1/1955, no known address in the bar. The three of them engaged in a conversation. It was not exactly known when they left, but all left together. They got in Ms. ████'s car, a 1980 Dodge Colt, Wisconsin License # NC 6492/80. They started to drive around the east side. While they were driving, the deceased and ████ started to argue. At this time, ████ hit the deceased alongside of his head. The deceased was seated in the right front seat and ████ in the rear seat. The deceased was angered by the blow, he reached in the back seat and pulled the assailent from the car. The deceased and Ms. ████ then went to the deceased's apartment. They fried some pork chops, ate and then engaged in a sexual involement. The deceased then complained of a headache. Ms. ████ gave the deceased some Tylenol. A short time past, the deceased's headache didnt get any better. Ms. ████ then drove the deceased to St. Marys hospital where he was admitted. Det. Tingue stated that the deceased works at Lakewood Nursing Home, 215 East Woodstock Pl. He left work at 9:00 PM on December 1, 1980. The police have been seeking other persons who know the assailant. The assailant is being sought by police. There will be a team sent for the autopsy with additional information.

J.T. Dubinski JTD

OVER

3420

Saturday December 6,80 8:00AM M. Panfil, B of I Milwaukee Police department came to this office and took 3 photos along with 3 right index prints of the subject. The prints match those on file for Michael Gerald ██████, DOB 12/30/49, B of I #152666.

R. Goeb *RG*

Saturday December 6,80 9:00AM Dr. J. Means called this office regarding Michael ██████, DOB 12/30/49. The doctor stated that he has been the ██████ Family Physican since the subject was about 12 years of age. The doctor stated that about 10 years ago the subject was in California working as a window washer. The subject was about three floors above the ground when the rope broke causing the subject to fall to the ground. The fall resulted in head and right arm injury for which he was confined to intensive care. The doctor stated that he will make his records available to this office if need be. The doctor also stated that the subject's mother who is confined to St. Michael Hospital has been made aware of the death.

R. Goeb *RG*

Saturday, 12/6/80, 2:05 PM: B of I Tech Panfil came to the morgue and took 3 color photographs of the deceased MICHAEL G. ██████.

John J. Guss *JJG*

Ex-employe quizzed in bow-and-arrow slaying

MILWAUKEE COUNTY MEDICAL EXAMINER

CASE NO. 2314

SUPPLEMENTARY

Name KARL [redacted]
Date Death 12/20/81

Sunday, 12/20/81, 9:25am, Capt. Hintz, Milwaukee Police Detective Bureau, called and reported to the undersigned the death of KARL [redacted], white male, age 44, of 2519 North [redacted].

He stated that the decedent had been shot in the abdomen with an arrow while on the street this morning. He stated that the incident occured at 3:45am, possibly in front of or near his home. A twenty year old suspect is in custody. He stated he was just called and informed by County General Hospital that the decedent had expired at 8:40am. He will have the investigating officers call this office with various details as now known about this case.

Inspector Will came on the line and stated he wanted the doctor on duty this date to be aware that following the decedent being shot by the arrow the paramedics were called to the scene. They refused to transport the decedent at once and the initial information at this time is that the paramedics stayed in the field with the decedent for well over an hour while the decedent bled out internally. He asked that the medical examiner be made aware of the paramedics possible complicity in the decedent's death.

J.R.Endrizzi

Sunday, December 20, 1981: 9:30AM: Received a call from Debbie ZANGL,RN, Milwaukee County General Hospital, reporting a death in the operating room. The deceased is Karl [redacted], white male, age unknown, address unknown. The deceased was admitted into the hospital via Paramed ambulance arriving at 5:00AM this date with an admitting diagnosis of arrow wound to the abdomen and multipal wounds to the bowels. Informant stated that the deceased had expired on the table diring the operation with the pronouncement being made at 8:40AM this date by Dr. Rahiman. Informant stated that they were advised that this would be listed as a homicide if the patient died as he had been shot by an X employee. A Medical Examiners hold was placed on the deceased pending additional investigation by this office.

William L. Harling

Sunday, 12/20/81, 10:05am, Detective Ballering, Squad 105 Late, called and stated that he and his partner, Det. Schoesscw, were working on this case. He stated that the deceased is KARL [redacted], white male, age 47, born 2/12/34, of 2519 North [redacted]. The address is a three family unit with the decedent being the owner. The decedent was single, never married, and lived alone at the residence. The other half of the building was occupied by the decedent's friend and bar manager, the decedent being the bar owner, and the bar managers mother. The bar manager is Ronald Peter [redacted], 2519B North [redacted], 6/12/36. This morning at 3:40am, [redacted] heard a pounding on his side door and answered finding the decedent wounded in the abdomen. The decedent stated to him;"Help me, Help me! Buzzy finally got me!"

[redacted] called for the paramedics who responded at once but did not convey. After working in the field with the deceased for an extended period of time.

The officers interviewed several persons who stated that Buzzy is one HERBERT [redacted]. W/M, 7/20/61, of 2831 South Wentworth, which address is that of a female friend with whom [redacted] is living at present. The officers went to that address and arrested [redacted] who has refused to comment on the case.

Information developed by the police indicates that the decedent was the owner of Oliver's Tavern, 782 North Milwaukee Street, and VonTriers Tavern, 2235 North Farwell. [redacted] was known to the decedent for more than two years, was an employee of the decedent's and was fired for cause some 6 months ago.

The arrow recovered at the scene is wooden, 30" in length,

(over)

continued

has a double barbed razor metal tip, and was broken into two parts on being found. When the break occured is unknown; whether on impact or following it's being imbedded in the decedent.

The undersigned called the Milwaukee Fire Department and spoke with FF. Lt. Ruthenberg. He obtained the run book and stated that the fire department was called for assistance at the scene this morning. The call to Med 5 was received as follows:

Call:	3:48am
Arrived scene:	3:52am
Departed scene:	4:20am
Arrived Hospital:	4:45am
Departed Hospital	5:10am

The firemen on the unit, Paramedic Unit #5 were Howard Sleva, Kenneth Covington, and driver Rodney Vidikovich.

Mr. Hill of this office called and was advised of the death. The medical examiner's ambulance, Milwaukee Conveyance, was called to make the removal from the hospital at 9:40am.

J.R.Endrizzi

Sunday, 12/20/81, 2:05pm, Ronald ██████, 2519B North ██████, 964-████, came to this office with Detective Kazuda. He viewed the body of the deceased and identified it as that of his employeer, KARL ██████.

He stated that his grandparents had acted as sponsors for the decedent when he emigrated to this country from Germany many years ago. The informant is now the decedent's manager at Olivers tavern.

This morning the informant was in bed with his wife when he heard the decedent outside crying out; "Zebby, Help Me!" This was repeated several times. The informant pulled on a pair of pants and went to see what was going on. He found the decedent continuing to cry out for help, using the same phrase. The decedent by this time had made it up the stairs to the apartment proper and stated; "Zebby, I'm shot. Buzzy got me." The words regarding Zebby I'm shot may have been Zebby I've been shot or some similar phrase, however, without question he stated to the informant; "Buzzy got me." The informant then called for help.

He stated that his aunt, Mrs. Thompson, had called Germany this morning and notified the decedent's father, step-mother, and other family members of the death. He stated that Buzzy is known to him as Herbert ██████.

J.R.Endrizzi

Monday, 12/21/81, 1:00pm, Det. Louis Bono came to the medical examiner's office and attended the autopsy of the decedent. He obtained at autopsy, from Dr. Samuels, the following items: shoes, socks, blue jeans, blet, and jockey shorts in a sealed brown paper bag; a selaed plastic bag with rectal swabs; sealed vial of blood; and ten sealed white paper envelopes with a nail and scrappings from each finger of each hand. These items were listed by the undersigned and were already in the detective's possession.

J.R.Endrizzi

Monday, 12/21/81, 5:15PM, PO Dave Gorecki of the B of I came to this office and took one full set of prints and two color photos, of KARL LOTHARIUS.

C. Borchardt

Sal Mineo

COUNTY OF LOS ANGELES

THOMAS T. NOGUCHI, M.D.
CHIEF MEDICAL EXAMINER-CORONER

12

AUTOPSY REPORT

No. 76-1953

I performed an autopsy on the body of MINEO, SAL

at DEPARTMENT OF CHIEF MEDICAL EXAMINER-CORONER

1104 N. MISSION RD., L.A. on FEBRUARY 13, 1976 (Date) @ 1200 Hours (Time)

From the anatomic findings and pertinent history I ascribe the death to:

(A) MASSIVE HEMORRHAGE

DUE TO OR AS A CONSEQUENCE OF

(B) STAB WOUND TO CHEST, PERFORATING THE HEART

DUE TO OR AS A CONSEQUENCE OF

(C)

OTHER SIGNIFICANT CONDITIONS–

Anatomical Summary:

I. FATAL STAB WOUND:

A. Stab wound to chest perforating the heart (Pictorial #1).

1. Hemorrhagic track, left 4th intercostal space, anterior pericardial sac, heart, through and through, posterior pericardial sac and inferior vena cava.
2. Massive hemopericardium, due to above.
3. Massive left hemothorax, due to above.
4. Atelectasis, left lung, due to above.

II. OTHER INJURIES:

A. Fresh abrasion, left gluteal region (Pictorial #2).

B. Fresh, small hemorrhage, subcutaneous tissue of scalp (Pictorial #4A).

III. OTHER CONDITIONS:

A. Intramuscular injection sites, right (x1) and left (x2) gluteal regions (Pictorial #2).

76A879M–Rev. 3/73)– Cdb 2-74

COUNTY OF LOS ANGELES

CASE REPORT

THOMAS T. NOGUCHI, M.D.
CHIEF MEDICAL EXAMINER-CORONER

1

Crypt # 103

Tape # 1-3A Start 518 End 560

REPORTED AS: [ ] Natural [X] Homicide [ ] In Custody [ ] Accident [ ] Undetermined [ ] Nursing Home [ ] Suicide [ ] At Work

6 1953
MINEO SAL
000 2 12 76
HOMICIDE 103

STAB WOUND TO (L) CHEST.

Case No. 76-1953 Taken by Shelton. Phone at Scene:

Post Mortem at C.M.E. Coroner. Request of

1a NAME OF DECEASED—FIRST NAME	1b MIDDLE NAME	1c LAST NAME	2a DATE OF DEATH—MONTH DAY YEAR	2b HOUR
SAL		MINEO	2-12-76	2155

3 SEX	4 COLOR OR RACE	5 BIRTHPLACE (STATE OR FOREIGN COUNTRY)	6 DATE OF BIRTH	7 AGE (LAST BIRTHDAY)	IF UNDER 1 YEAR	IF UNDER 24 HOURS
Male	Cauc		1-10-39	37 YEARS		

8. NAME AND BIRTHPLACE OF FATHER	9 MAIDEN NAME AND BIRTHPLACE OF MOTHER

10 CITIZEN OF WHAT COUNTRY	11 SOCIAL SECURITY NUMBER	12 MARRIED NEVER MARRIED WIDOWED DIVORCED (SPECIFY)	13 NAME OF SURVIVING SPOUSE (IF WIFE ENTER MAIDEN NAME)

14 LAST OCCUPATION	15 NUMBER OF YEARS IN THIS OCCUPATION	16 NAME OF LAST EMPLOYING COMPANY OR FIRM (IF SELF EMPLOYED, SO STATE)	17 KIND OF INDUSTRY OR BUSINESS

18a PLACE OF DEATH—NAME OF HOSPITAL OR OTHER IN PATIENT FACILITY	18b STREET ADDRESS—(STREET AND NUMBER OR LOCATION)	18c INSIDE CITY CORPORATE LIMITS (SPECIFY YES OR NO)
	Rear 8567 Holloway Dr. WLA.	yes

18d CITY OR TOWN	18e COUNTY	18f LENGTH OF STAY IN COUNTY OF DEATH	18g LENGTH OF STAY IN CALIFORNIA
W. LA.	LA	YEARS	YEARS

19a USUAL RESIDENCE—STREET ADDRESS (STREET AND NUMBER OR LOCATION)	19b INSIDE CITY CORPORATE LIMITS (SPECIFY YES OR NO)	20 NAME AND MAILING ADDRESS OF INFORMANT
8569 HOLLOWAY DR APT. 1	yes	

19c CITY OR TOWN	19d COUNTY	19e STATE
W.L.A.	LA	Cal.

Reported by RASURE Address LASO Phone

Date 2-13-76 Time 0016 Pronounced Dead by RA 7

Investigating Agency LASO HOMI + CORONER Officer SGT. PIA.

Date Time Hospital No. Religion

Next of Kin JOSEPHINE MINEO Address 83 WEST ST. HARRISON, N.Y.

Relationship MOTHER Phone Notified by LASO. yes Date and Time 2-13-76

Personal I.D. By: Address

City Relationship Phone Initials and Date

DPSS Case Number
Vet. [ ] Yes [ ] No
C#
SERIAL #
Brought in by Baker
Date and Time 2-13-76 0220

Prints [X] Yes [ ] No
Property [X] Yes [ ] No
Clothing [X] Yes [ ] No
Door Sealed [ ] Yes [X] No

Weight 149 lbs.
Height 68 In.
Hair Blk
Eyes Brn
U.
Teeth L.

Mustache no
Beard no
Tattoo no
Deformity no
Body Condition STAB WOUND (L) CHEST. Viewable

Baker Deputy

33 SPECIFY ACCIDENT SUICIDE OR HOMICIDE	34 PLACE OF INJURY (SPECIFY HOME, FARM, FACTORY, STREET, OFFICE BUILDING, ETC.)	35 INJURY AT WORK (SPECIFY YES OR NO)	36a DATE OF INJURY—MONTH DAY YEAR	36b HOUR
HOMICIDE	ALLEY	no	2-12-76	2130 hrs.

37a PLACE OF INJURY (STREET AND NUMBER OR LOCATION AND CITY OR TOWN)	37b DISTANCE FROM PLACE OF INJURY TO USUAL RESIDENCE (ITEM 19)	38 WERE LABORATORY TESTS DONE FOR DRUGS OR TOXIC CHEMICALS (SPECIFY YES OR NO)	39 WERE LABORATORY TESTS DONE FOR ALCOHOL (SPECIFY YES OR NO)
REAR 8567 HOLLOWAY DR W.L.A.	0 MILES	YES	YES

40 DESCRIBE HOW INJURY OCCURRED (ENTER SEQUENCE OF EVENTS WHICH RESULTED IN INJURY. NATURE OF INJURY SHOULD BE ENTERED IN ITEM 29)
AS ABOVE BY UNKNOWN PERSON.(S)

Assigned to Dr. CERTIFICATE MADE DEFERRED [ ] By FINAL [ ] By

CERTIFICATE ISSUED: TO MORTUARY DEFERRED By FINAL By RDS 2-13-76

76C108B4 - (REV. 7/73) (1-72) - Cdb 6-75

COUNTY OF LOS ANGELES

MEDICAL REPORT

THOMAS T. NOGUCHI, M.D.
CHIEF MEDICAL EXAMINER-CORONER

15

Date FEB 13, 1976 Time 1200 HRS IN ☒ OUT ☐

Crypt # ______ MORTUARY Co. L. Coroner

☐ INVESTIGATION ☒ AUTOPSY ☐ PENDING

☒ FINAL ON FEB 13, 1976 Dr. M. R. DHETON, MD

76 1953
MIWEO SAL
000 2 12 76
HOMICIDE 103

PART I: DEATH WAS CAUSED BY:
IMMEDIATE CAUSE

MASSIVE HEMORRHAGE

Due to:

STAB WOUND TO CHEST, PERFORATING THE HEART

Due to:

☐ Micro ☐ Neuro
☐ Bact. ☐ Med. History
☐ P. R. ☐ S.P.R.
☐ Photo By ______
☐ X-ray ☒ A.S. Photo 1
☒ Toxicology ☐ Smears
☒ Alcohol ☐ Over 24 Hrs.
☒ Barbs. ☐ C O
☒ Other – Explain Below
NARCO

PART II: OTHER SIGNIFICANT CONDITIONS - CONTRIBUTING TO DEATH BUT NOT RELATED TO THE IMMEDIATE CAUSE GIVEN IN PART I.

SPECIMENS SUBMITTED
☒ Kidney ☒ Bile
☒ Liver ☒ Urine
☒ Stomach ☒ Other INJECTION SITES
☒ Yes – Explain PERIPHERAL VEINS

☐ NATURAL ☐ ACCIDENT ☐ SUICIDE ☒ HOMICIDE ☐ UNDETERMINED

Operation – ☐ Yes ☒ No Evidence of Injury – ☒ Yes ☐ No At work – ☐ Yes ☒ No

Suicide note – ☐ Yes ☒ No Evidence brought in None

Embalmed by: ______ License No. ______ Blood Sample Taken ☐ No –

R_x No. None Date Filled: ______ Contents: ______ Amount Prescribed: ______ Amount Remaining: ______

PHYSICAL DESCRIPTION Age 37 Sex Male Race Cauc Complexion Med. Wt. 144 lbs. Ht. 68 in.

Hair Blk Teeth U/L ____ Eyes Brn Pupils Eq Scars, amputations, Stab wound (L) chest.

Appliances on body, Surgical wounds None Tattoo or deformity ______

Hospital Report – ☐ Yes ☒ No Hospitalized In N/A Hospital Duration ______

For ______ Information taken by Baska Date 2-13-76

MEDICAL EXAMINER'S COMMENTS AND/OR PERTINENT AUTOPSY FINDINGS:

I.D. by ______ [signature] M.D.

CERTIFICATE ISSUED Pending ☐ FINAL ☒ Signed ☐ By RDS 2-13-76

WHITE – FILE COPY
PINK – TOXICOLOGY COPY
GREEN – TOXICOLOGY COPY
YELLOW – PHYSICIAN'S COPY
BLUE – MEDICAL EXAMINER COPY

76M118T – (Rev. 1/74) – Cdb 3-74

COUNTY OF LOS ANGELES

CASE REPORT

THOMAS T. NOGUCHI, M.D.
CHIEF MEDICAL EXAMINER-CORONER

3

CONTINUATION SHEET

Case No.
Case Name 76 1953
NINEO SAL
DOD 2 12 76
HOMICIDE 103
Date

INFO FROM SGT. PIA LASO AT SCENE 2/13/76 0125 hrs

AT APPROXIMATELY 2130 HRS. 2/12/76, CRIES FOR HELP WERE HEARD, BY TENENTS, FROM REAR OF 8567 HOLLOWAY DR. W. LOS ANGELES

L.A CO. SHERIFFS OFFICE WAS ALERTED AND UNITS RESPONDED TO REAR OF 8567 HOLLOWAY DR. W.L.A. AND FOUND DECEDENT ON HIS SIDE, IN FETAL POSITION, IN DRIVEWAY BETWEEN CARPORTS R7 AND R6 WITH STAB WOUND TO LEFT CHEST.

FIRE RESCUE UNIT 7 RESPONDED, TURNED DECEDENT ON HIS BACK, CUT JACKET AND SHIRT and attempted RESUSCITATION. DECEDENT PRONOUNCED DEAD AT 2155 HRS.

THIS INVESTIGATOR AND JAMES NJAVRO, CORONERS PHOTOGRAPHER, RESPONDED TO THE SCENE 2/13/76 AT 0125 HRS. PHOTOGRAPHED DECEDENT AND SEARCHED BODY.

DECEDENTS WALLET, CONTAINING $21.00 IN BILLS FOUND IN LEFT JACKET POCKET. YELLOW METAL POCKET WATCH WITH CHAIN IN RT. JACKET POCKET. COINS IN LEFT PANTS POCKET. 85CENTS IN CHANGE FOUND ON PAVEMENT UNDER DECEDENT. WHITE METAL RING NOTED ON DECEDENTS LEFT INDEX FINGER AND LEFT ON BODY.

SEVERAL RESTAURANT RECEIPT STUBS AND 2 CARDS WITH NAMES AND PHONE NUMBERS FOUND IN DECEDENTS POCKETS AND WERE RETAINED BY SGT. PIA FOR FURTHER INVESTIGATION.

DECEDENTS HANDS WERE BAGGED AT THE SCENE FOR PROTECTION FOR SHERIFFS CRIME LAB.

DECEDENTS BODY FOUND IN EAST WEST POSITION WITH HEAD TOWARD THE EAST.

NO WEAPON FOUND AT SCENE AND NO SUSPECTS IN CUSTODY AT THIS TIME.

DECEDENTS AUTOMOBILE NOTED PARKED IN CAR PORT AT REAR OF HIS APARTMENT #1 8569 HOLLOWAY DR. A SHORT DISTANCE WEST OF WHERE DECEDENT WAS FOUND.

2-13-76 0530 hrs Autopsy scheduled for 1200 hrs. Please alert police. Thanks [initials]

Barker
INVESTIGATOR

2-13-76
DATE

WHITE - FILE
YELLOW - TOXICOLOGY
PINK - INVESTIGATIONS

App 2-13-76 [signature]

76M110U - (REV. 4/73) - CM 2/74

Man kills self in Russian Roulette game

MILWAUKEE COUNTY MEDICAL EXAMINER

CASE NO. 1074

SUPPLEMENTARY

Name BRUCE ████
Date Death 6/8/79

Friday, 6/8/79, 5:15pm, Lt. Schoberg, Milwaukee Police District #2, called and reported that officers from his department were at the intersection of East Howard and South Pine where the body of an obviously dead white male was discovered. He requested and investigator and ambulance be dispatched to the scene.

Medical Examiner's Ambulance dispatched at 5:20pm.

The undersigned was met at the scene by Detectives Hass and Nowicki, Squad 112 early, and several uniform officers. The detectives stated that the vehicle in question, a 1973 Oldsmobile 2 door, black over gold, 1979 Wisconsin license QX 9616, was westbound on Howard when the auto stopped for a red light at south Pine Street. The vehicle was in the right driving lane. The vehicle was being driven by DOUGLAS CHARLES ████, W/M, 1/12/58, of ████ South 76th Street, 259-████. He was not the owner of the vehicle. Seated in the passengers seat was BRUCE ████, white male, age 27, address unknown, who was the owner of the vehicle and a friend, for the past 2½ years of ████. ████ stated to the officers that while stopped at the light, the decedent reached under the right front seat, pulled out a gun case, unzipped the case, removed from the case a revolver, opened the cylinder of the revolver, inserted one round, closed the cylinder, spun the cylinder, placed the muzzle against his head, and pulled the trigger. The weapon discharged fatally wounding the decedent. ████ stated that he and the decedent had been at ████'s home where they had been smoking marijuana. They then decided to drive to northern Wisconsin, packed the car, drove to a near-by grocery store where they bought a 12-pack of beer, and began their journey. They had gone only a few blocks before the incident occured. ████ had been removed from the scene and had been taken to the Detective Bureau when the undersigned arrived.

The undersigned then made a cursory examination of the decedent, who was still seated inside the vehicle. He is seen to be seated in the right seat of this two door car which has bucket seats. A massive head wound is observed which has evacuated the cranial vault. Tissue and blood cover the right front portion of the vehicle-inside. A "spray pattern" is noted to the front and right of where the decedent is seated. Blood, tissue and bone fragments are on the floor, seat, and dash. Directly above the decedent the headliner is noted to be without blood or tissue "spray". Blood is noted to the right window, door panel, and right rear window. Found in the glove compartment are several boxes of ammunition including W-W .357 magnum rounds. Five rounds of this type were found on the floor between the decedent's three of the rounds are exposed to view and two are found under brain matter. Beer in a styrofoam cooler, clothing, empty beer cans, and a clip for a .223 calibre rifle were found in the back seat. In the trunk officers found a covered AR-15 rifle with scope. These items were removed by the officers as was a revolver found on the lap of the decedent; a COLT TROOPER .357 MAGNUM blue steel with wood grips. The right hand was about the grip of the weapon, however, the finger(s) were not through the trigger guard. The weapon had obvious fingerprints and was not opened to see how many rounds it contained nor was the serial number obtained due to tissue on the weapon and the desire not to disturb the prints until the weapon could be processed by the BofI, MPD. The medical examiner's ambulance conveyed the body from the scene, the doors being locked there by the undersigned.

J.R.Endrizzi

Friday, 6/8/79, 7:45pm, Detective Nowicki brought the brother of the decedent, BRUCE K. ████, to the county morgue where he identified the decedent as his brother. The undersigned then interviewed the brother, Craig ████, W/M, 2/14/58, of

continued

████ South Kansas. He stated that his brother and ████ were good friends and had arrived at the informant's home at approximately 4:00pm this date. He did not know who was driving at the time. They arrived in the decedent's car. They entered to talk about their up coming weekend. The parents of the informant own a trailer which is parked on a lot in Endeavor, WISC, which is located approximately 19 miles west of Portage. The father had already gone to the trailer to begin work on it as it had been damaged by the elements during the winter. The decedent and Wilke were to work on the trailer during the week end with the father and they were to be joined on Saturday evening by the informant.

The informant stated that on arrival at his home this date the decedent brought into his home a blue steel revolver. He, the decedent and ████ all handled the weapon. The informant opened the cylinder and noted that the weapon was empty. He then dry fired the weapon several times. The informant then drank a beer while Wilke and the decedent split one beer between them. The informant then asked them if they wanted to smoke some marijuana. They stated they did and he produced "two joints" which they all shared. The gun was placed in a zipper case by ████ and removed from the home by one of the two; ie either ████ or the decedent. The decedent asked ████ to drive and he did so. Shortly thereafter the informant left his home enroute to his place of employment. As he approached the intersection of Pine and Howard he observed the decedent's car parked in the right traffic lane. ████ was standing outside the vehicle. The informant thought they had car trouble and stopped to help. ████ then approached the informant and stated; "Bruce shot himself." The informant looked inside the car, saw the gun on his brother's lap and saw the wound which had been produced. The paramedics then arrived.

The informant stated that his brother had been in the Marine Corps and had recently seen the movie "The Deer Hunter" a film based on events which occured during the Vietnam War. In the film some of the characters play Russian Roulette. Since seeing the film the decedent has on several occasion spun the cylinder of the weapon, placed it to his head, and dry fired the weapon. He never had placed a round in the gun and never gave indications of depression or intent to take his life. Several times he had placed a gum wrapper in one of the cylinders, closed the cylinder, and fired the weapon while the muzzel was placed against his right temple. He played this way in the presence of others including his girlfriend, Susan ████, W/F, 9/26/55, of ████ West Morgan, to whom he was to be married in July 1979. She objected to these displays, and so, the incidents of such play had become more infrequent. The decedent had seen the movie in question several times and the brother stated, that the deceased had never prior to seeing the movie ever acted out such strange behavior. The brother stated that as the decedent had never before placed a live round in the weapon, and as the decedent had never indicated any intention to take his own life, he feels that ████ placed the round in the weapon unbeknownst to the decedent; either as a joke or with the intention of having the decedent kill or seriously injure himself. He stated that the decedent had no medical problems, had a secure job with good wages, had no history of mental problems, no history of suicidal episodes, and had made no threats against himself. The decedent had no enemies, no one had threatened him with harm, and the informant does not think anyone would have caused him harm as the decedent was a black belt karate instructor at the YUN Black Belt Academy.

The undersigned then went to the Milwaukee Police Department Detective Bureau and interviewed Mr. ████. ████ was clad in blue jean cut-off slacks, tennis shoes and a white t-shirt. The right hand portion of the shirt and cut-offs were blood splattered, consistant with his statement that he was driving the vehicle when the weapon was discharged. He stated to the undersigned that the decedent had driven the car to the informants's home on 6/7/79 in the evening. He asked the informant to do several small jobs and run several erzands for him this date. Because of this he left his car with the informant. The informant was told to

continued

MILWAUKEE COUNTY MEDICAL EXAMINER

CASE NO. 1074

SUPPLEMENTARY 2

Name BRUCE K. █████
Date Death 6/8/79

continued

to meet the decedent at the home of the decedent's girlfriend at 3:30pm this date. █████ arrived at the home, █████ West Morgan, at 3:20pm this date. The decedent had driven his motorcycle to work and had parked the bike at the girlfriends home for the week-end. The decedent invited Wilke in and after 15 or 20 minutes they loaded the car with clothing and food for their trip to Endeavor. They then finished the beer they had been drinking, loaded an AR-15 into the trunk, and it was at that point that the decedent produced the revolver. █████ picked up the weapon, opened the cylinder, found it empty, and dry fired the gun. The decedent then placed the gun in a zipper case and the gun was then carried to the car; the informant can not recall who carried the weapon to the car. They then drove to Don Striker's Gun Shop, 2465 South 84th Street, where they entered the shop and purchased one 20 round box of .223 calibre ammunition for the AR-15. No other ammunition was purchased. They then drove to the decedent's residence, █████ South 46th Street, where the decedent went in alone. He picked up several items including various boxes of ammunition. These items were placed on the back seat and in the glove compartment. They then drove to Craig █████'s home, █████ South Kansas. They both entered, the decedent bringing with him the Colt Trooper they had been playing with before. Again the weapon wasn handled by the informant and the decedent and was also handled by Craig. The weapon was again seen by █████ to be empty. They smoked some marijuana, drank beer, and then left; the decedent asking █████ to drive. They then drove to the Open Pantry Food Store, 1141 East Howard, where the decedent exited the vehicle to shop while Wilke waited in the car. He stated that he then took the weapon, which was in the zipper case, and placed in on the floor of the front seat area. He stated he did this so that no one would see the gun case. The decedent returned to the auto with the 12 pack of beer, chips, dip, and ice he had purchased. The ice and beer were placed in the cooler on the rear seat and they drove off; the informant driving. They had driven a short distance when the decedent reached down, took out the gun case, unzipped the case, and removed the gun. At this point the informant's story is rather sketchie. He stated that he observed the decedent take the gun, open the cylinder, take out a box of rounds from the glove compartment, load the revolver with six rounds, close the cylinder, and then reopen the cylinder. The decedent then took out all six rounds and then placed one round back in the cylinder. The informant then observed him spin the cylinder, place the muzzle to his right temple and pull the trigger. The gun discharged while they were stopped at the red light westbound on Howard at Pine. The informant turned off the engine and ran to a near-by house for help.

The informant also stated that he did not see exactly what the decedent had been doing and had seen him, out of the corner of his eye, spin the cylinder, place the gun to his head, and fire. He stated that he really did not pay attention to what the decedent was doing. His statement at this point were somewhat evasive and his recounting of the events was somewhat disjointed. The informant was lucid, alert, and appeared to be in full possession of his faculties. He did not appear confused, rather, evasive. On all other points he was most specific. He denied that he placed the round in the weapon as a joke or with the intention of seeing the decedent injured/killed.

Mr. Hill was contacted and ordered the body held for autopsy.

J.R.Endrizzi

MILWAUKEE COUNTY MEDICAL EXAMINER

CASE NO. 1694

SUPPLEMENTARY

Name EULICE [redacted]
Date Death September 11, 1981

September 11,1981, Friday, 3:35 AM.

Detective Captain Perlewitz, called this office to report a shooting at 2819 North [redacted] Street. He requests an investigator and conveyance at the scene. Thomas F. Hanratty dispatched. Medical Examiner's Ambulance sent at 3:40 AM.

E. Himmelreich EH

Friday September 11, 1981; 3:55AM

Drove to [redacted] North 20th Street, an upper flat in the heart of an economically depressed neighborhood in the predominantly Black community of the inner city. Was met at the scene by Detective Lieutenant CRAIG HASTING, Detectives FRED ULLRICH and SINCERE, other detectives and several uniformed officers. Was shown to the rear hallway, downstairs, where a chalk outline of a body can be seen just inside the rear outside door. The body of an adult Black male can be seen about 15 feet North of the chalk outline, down a short hallway, inside an unfurnished room. The body had been placed in this room by the Paramedics, who had found the body wedged against the outer door, in the hallway. The subject was shot in the head while on the stairs leading to the upstairs apartment, had tumbled down into the hall and became wedged against the door. The call had come into the Fire Department at 3:13AM and the Paramedics made the death pronouncement at 3:30AM.

A cursory examination of the body reveals it to be an adult Black male, later identified as EULICE REED [redacted], 27 years old, DOB 8/2/1954, of this residence. The body is lying face up, dressed in a beige silken nightgown. The finger and toe nails are colored red and the hair is prepared in numerous small braids. A large amount of blood can be seen to the head, with a pool of blood in the outer hallway. An apparent gunshot entrance wound of a medium to large caliber is noted to the the left side of the head, just behind the left ear. The body is warm and no stiffness can be detected in either the jaw or any extremities. The room temperature is 76 degrees and a rectal temperature taken at 4:10AM is 99 degrees. No other wound is apparent.

Checked the stairs leading to the upstairs apartment. There are 10 steps, with 8" risers and 9" treads, 36" wide. Five of the wooden stairs have metal strips and blood splashes or pools are noted on the lower three steps, as well as the lower hallway. No blood is seen either in the apartment or the upper landing. A door off of the upper landing leads to a closet containing mostly female garments. A second door off of the upper landing leads to the three room upper flat. Papers found in the upper flat indicate the name and date of birth of the deceased. In addition, one of the officers at the scene stated that he and his partner had been to the residence a week or so ago in response to a disturbance complaint and had interviewed the deceased who gave the name "Sandra Reed". A pill vial containing six white scored tablets was found in the bedroom of the flat and is labeled "Percocet" with the name EULICE [redacted], but gives the sex as "F". The label is from Milwaukee County General Hospital and gives a patient number as 54 21 09 8, and a date of birth as 8/2/54. An identification card issued to Eulice [redacted] shows a picture of the deceased made up and dressed as a female.

When the police arrived at the scene this morning, no weapon or suspect was found, although the police pursued at least one possible suspect who fled on foot. Prowl cars are combing the neighborhood looking for suspects, and other witnesses are being interviewed. Details of the deceased's lifestyle and habits are being sought by the police at this time. The body was removed by the DAVIS brothers of Milwaukee Conveyers.

Thomas F. Hanratty TFH

(over)

3420

9/11/81 - 7:05 AM

B of I Tech.A. DeStafano came to this office and took three colored photos, and performed GSR tests on the deceased. The deceased's right index fingerprint was taken. The fingerprint matched that on file, B of I #135309, Samuel Lee ████, dob-8/2/1954.

E.Himmelreich EH

Friday, September 11, 1981: 1:05PM: Received a return call from Barbara, at Medical Records, Milwaukee County General Hospital, in reference to additional information on the deceased, Eulice ████. Informant stated that the deceased is lised as a female, with a husband listed as Charles, of the same address as deceased, phone (414-449████). The records show that the deceased's father is Leroy and mother, Lillie of Indinia address and phone unknown. The deceased lists the maiden name as SAMUEL. The deceased was seen as an out-patient on 8-25-81 in the oral surgery clinic. The deceased listed asthma as the only problem. There is no additional information.

William L. Harling WLH

Friday September 11,81 2:35PM D. Monfre B of I Milwaukee Police Department came to this office and took two photos of the deceased Samuel Lee ████, DOB 8/2/54.

R. Goeb RG

Friday September 11,81 3:00PM Marilyn ████, DOB 1/05/66, 2208 W. ████-2567 came to this office and identified the body as that of her cousin Samuel Lee ████, DOB 8/2/54. The informant stated that she last saw the subject yesterday afternoon at which time there was an altercation between the subject and a woman in a local grocery store. The informant stated that she did not hear anything to indicate ill feelings at the residence itself nor does she have any information pertaining to the events of last evening.

R. Goeb RG

Saturday, September 12, 1981: 8:58PM: Mr. Le Roy ████, black male, age, 54, date of birth, 8-24-27, of 244 ████, Hammond, Indiana, no phone, father of the deceased, Eulice ████ came to the County Morgue, with his sister, Ruby ████, of 834 ████ Street, Hammond, phone (219-████-9278), to get additional information on the deceased and to make identificati Informant was advised that this office had been told by Marion HARRIS, of the House of HARRIS that the Funeral Home had permission to remove the deceased's body for the family by the deceased s sister, Ruby. Informant LeRoy stated that his daughter Ruby ████ was in the hospital and could not have given permission to the House of harris and that they were informed that the body would be at the County Morgue. The family had engaged the HINTON and WILLIAM Funeral Home, 4859 Alexander Avenue, East Chicago, for this. Informant LeRoy stated that the deceased was last seen by the family in July of this year in Hammond, and, at that time, he had no illness of any type. The deceased had been discharged from the U.S.Navy with a dishonorable discharge. The family stated that as far as was known, the deceased was not taking any type of drugs nor smoking pot. The family will contact the House of Harris and also get the deceased's possessions from his residence. Informant LeRoy advised that he worked right in the Hammond Police Station, and any calls there should have been reported to him as everyone there knew him.

William L. Harling WLH

Woman killed when gun in briefcase discharges

MILWAUKEE COUNTY MEDICAL EXAMINER

CASE NO. ..282........

SUPPLEMENTARY

Name Mary ████
Date Death February 2,79

Friday February 2,79 7:45AM PO Johnson, Milwaukee Police Department called this office and requested an investigator be dispatched to 2963 N. Humboldt.
7:50AM R.L. Goeb dispatched to the above address.
8:05AM The undersigned arrived at the Tri-Power Service Station located at 2963 N. Humboldt and was met by Lt. Tisdale, Det. Damke and Koepke along with several uniform officers of the Milwaukee Police Department. The officers stated that they were called at 7:25AM by Gary J.████, DOB 11/3/50, 4313 N.███ St., 464-████, the owner of the station who claimed that there had been a shooting. The undersigned spoke with Mr. ████ who stated that he has known Mary E. ████,████ N. Dousman, DOB 2/1/49 as a customer for the past 6 months. Yesterday, 2/1/79, the subject left her car at the station for service because of starting problems. The subject returned her car this morning for more service. The informant stated that he arrived at the station at about 7:00AM. Upon his arrival the subject placed his briefcase on the counter located behind the service desk and went to the back room where the safe is located. The informant stated that he opened the safe to obtain the receipts from the night before. The informant returned to the service desk to place the monies in his briefcase when Ms. ████ came into the station. The informant stated that the subject gave him the car keys and he turned around the obtain a piece of paper in order to take the subject's phone number for the 8th Street School where she is employed as a teacher. As the informant did this the subject turned toward the door to look for Karon████,████ N. Bartlet, DOB 3/28/52,a friend, who was to take her to work. The informant stated that in turning he knocked his briefcase off the counter. The briefcase contained a Ruger .41 Magnum, #8270 which had been left as a security deposit by a customer. The weapon discharged after striking the floor with the projectile striking Ms. ████.

Examination of the weapon reveals it to be a single action revolver which is fully loaded with 6 .41 magnum, semi wadcutter, semi jacketed ammunition. Five of the cartridges are loaded.One spent cartridge is located under the hammer. Examination of the ammunition reveals that all six primers show signs of scratching and indentation from the firing pin. The weapon struck the floor about 4 feet behind the frontof the service desk. The projectile went through part of a 1" X4" particle board frame, and a piece of paneling prior to striking the subject. The projectile continued upward striking the ceiling 6' east of the service desk and 10'5" above the floor level. The body itself is on the floor in a supine position with her head to the north and feet to the south. The subject is fully dressed in a coat, blouse, skirt, shoes and stockings. To the right lower back of the coat there is an area of smudging about 1" in diameter. To the center of this there is a small defect in the material. This corresponds to a circular skin defect to the lower right posterior aspect of the body. There is another skin defect to the upper left anterior aspect of the body. No further visible signs of external trauma can be detected. The Medical Examiners Ambulance arrived and the body was conveyed to the County Morgue.

R. Goeb

Friday February 2,1979 12:15 PM: Mrs. Leo Dan ████ of ████ North Fredrick phone # ███-8025 came to this office. Informant and the undersigned viewed the remains. Mr. ████ identified the deceased as his wife of six years - Mary E. ████.
Informant requested that the undersigned contact the eye bank for him. Informant signed a donor request card and the undersigned contacted the Lions Eye Bank.
At 12:45PM the eyes were removed by Dr. Kinziger of County Hospital.

David W. Livingston

3420

Man commits suicide after shooting friend in gunplay

MILWAUKEE COUNTY MEDICAL EXAMINER

CASE NO. 98

SUPPLEMENTARY

Name DIANE L. [redacted]
Date Death January 12, 1980

11:42 PM - Saturday - January 12, 1980 - PHYLLIS POHLMAN, R.N., St. Luke's Hospital, called this office to report the death of DIANE L. [redacted], 2-20-56, marital status unknown, a resident of 3518 W. [redacted], Franklin, Wis.
Franklin Rescue Squad brought subject to the hospital from an unkjown location.
Dr. LAUFENBERG made the DOA pronouncement at 11:03 this PM.
On arrival at the hospital subject was fully clad for outdoor wear.
The body was warm and limp.
There is an apparent bullet entrance wound to the mid forehead with an apparent bullet exit wound to the back of the head.
Details of how this injury was suatained are unknown to the informant.
The body will be held at the hospital pending instructions from this office.

J.Kortsch JK

1/13/80, 12:05 AM

Contacted Franklin Police and spoke to PO. Nelson, who states that what.ever happened tonight, occurred at the Parkland Pub, 5621 West Rawson. A Sgt Scott, will stand by at the scene.

E.Himmelreich EH

1/13/80, 12:15 AM

Phyllis Pohlmann RN, at St Luke's Hospital, called this office. She states that the deceased's brother, Paul [redacted] (no other info) had been to the hospital, where he indentified both bodies(#98-97) at 12:10 AM, date.

1/13/80, 12:35 AM.

PO. Schenk #45, Franklin Police, called this office for permission to remove some items from the clothing of [redacted], case #97. Permission was denied, pending further knowledge of what happened this evening. Preliminary investigation, according to the informant, discloses the fact that at about 10:30 PM, at the Parkland Pub, 5621 West Rawson Avenue, the deceased Diane L. [redacted] and her cousin STEVEN R. [redacted] case #97, were sitting at the bar of this establishment. Steven took out a Ruger, 44 mag,"Super Blackhawk" single action revolver, from a holster on his belt, supposedly in a joking manner. A short time later a shot was heard and Diane was struck in the head by a bullet. A little later witnesses supposedly saw Steven [redacted] aim the weapon at his own head and pull the trigger. There were 4 live rounds and 2 spent rounds, one spent round under the hammer, of the cylinder of the weapon. The weapon is in police custody. Wittnesses are still being questioned. Detective Loomis , Franklin PD is in charge.

E.Himmelreich EH

1/13/80, 12:45 AM.

Medical Examiner's Ambulance sent for body removal per William L. Harling's, investigator, instructions.

E.Himmelreich EH

(OVER)

3420

(Cont.)

Sunday, January 13, 1980: 12:25AM: Arrived at the PARKLAND PUB, 5621 West Rawson Avenue, Franklin, which is located in a rural type area on the South side of the street. This is a one story construction type building with a single large area to the North and a bar along the South wall area. The undersigned was met at that location by Sgt. SCOTT, Squad # 48 and Det. Daniel LOOMIS, Squad # 41, both of the Franklin police department. The undersigned's attention was directed by Det. LOOMIS to the Southwest corner of the bar where it is observed a large pool of blood alongside a jukebox which is located along the West wall approximately 2 feet North of the Southwest corner of the bar. Informant stated that there were two persons involved in what appears to be an accidental shooting and suicide. Informant stated that the female was identified as Diane L. █████, white female, age, 23 date of birth, 2-20-56, of 3518 West █████, Franklin, phone unknown, and the male was identified as Steven R. █████, white male, age, 24 date of birth, 2-9-55, of █████ South Kinnickinnic, phone unknown. Informant stated that both bodies had been removed from the scene by the Franklin Fire Department and taken to St. Lukes Hospital prior to his arrival. Informant stated that from information received, the male and female were cousins who had entered the bar at approximately 9:30PM on 1-12-80. Informant stated that both had arrived in an auto belonging to the male. Informant stated that when they had arrived it appeared that both had been drinking. Informant stated that the female had taken the bar stool closest to the Southwest wall and the male sat to her immediate left. Informant stated that both had ordered and had been drinking Pabst beers. Informant stated that they were laughing and joking between themselves and there was no indication that they were arguing. Informant stated that there had been 6 other male patrons in the bar and a male bartender. Informant and the undersigned interviewed the bartender, Gregory █████, white male, age, 24 date of birth, 2-5-55, of █████ South 19th Court, phone (761-█████). Informant stated that he has been tending bar at the above location since November, 1979 and had seen both of the deceased's in the bar approximately 4-5 times. Informant stated that he had been down at the East end of the bar with his back to the deceased's at approximately 10:30PM when he heard a loud noise sounding like a M-80 firecracker going off. Informant stated that he had turned and started to walk to where the deceased's were sitting when he observed the female laying on her back with her head toward the jukebox and her feet toward the bar. Informant stated that at that time he had also observed the male standing up facing West with his left hand raised in an approximate 70 degree angle toward the ceiling and what appeared to be a revolver in his left hand. Informant stated that the male did not say a word and within a few seconds the male had raised the revolver to his left temple and had fired one shot. Informant stated that the male had then fell forward and his body covered that of the female with the gun between the bodies. Informant stated that he was stunned for a while and then had called the police department. Informant stated that after the shooting and prior to the police arriving two of the male patrons had ran out of the bar. Informant had no knowledge of the names of these males. Informant Det. LOOMIS stated that all of the bar patrons who had been in the bar were presently at the Franklin Police Department giving statements

Futher investigation by the undersigned indicated that from information given the female body was in a supine position with the head against the jukebox to the Northwest and her feet were to the Southeast. The male was laying across the female in an "L" shape with the head to the Southwest and the feet to the South. Measurements taken were as follows: bar along the South side measures 23 feet 9 inches in length at which point it curves from a direction to the East to a point directly to the South. The bar stools have been moved however the beer that the female was drinking was 5 feet East of the West wall and the beer that the male was drinking was 5 feet 8 inches East of the West wall. The jukebox is 3 feet to the North of the bar and against the West wall. The distance from the West wall to the East wall is 39 feet 2 inches. There is a section of paneling missing from the West wall at a height of 7 feet 1 inch and approximately 3 1/2 feet North of the bar. From the approximate location given as to the position of the male a distance of 16 feet 9 inches at an approximate 30 degree angle was measured to an apparent exit hole in a plexiglass type window. the window is approximately 1/8 inch thick. It is noted

MILWAUKEE COUNTY MEDICAL EXAMINER

CASE NO. ..98..........

SUPPLEMENTARY # 2

Name Diane L. ████████
Date Death 1-12-80

here that there are three additional holes in the window that appear to be from other shooting incidents and have been plugged up. Futher investigation revealed a spent missile appearing to be .44 cal. in size. The missile is located on the floor 1 1/2 feet from the East wall and 9 feet 2 inches from the front door on the Northeast side of the building. Inspection of the missile shows traces of what appear to be wood imbedded in it. Closer inspection reveals an area appearing to be indented from the missile striking the East wall sideways that is 6 feet 10 inches from the floor and 9 feet 3 inches from the Northeast corner.

Information received from Sgt. SCOTT of the Franklin police department indicated that the deceased's car contained two boxes of ammunition. The ammunition was on the front seat. One box was 1/2 empty and contained .44 cal. Magnum Remington rounds. The other box was full and it contained .44 cal. Special Smith and Wesson rounds. Informant stated that the deceased male's jacket also contained an unknown amount of spent shell casings in the pocket. The weapon used was listed as a Ruger Blackhawk revolver, .44 magnum with a 7 inch barrel bearing serial number 82-92844. The weapon has two spent rounds and 4 live rounds in it. There is a spent round under the hammer and in line with the bore. The weapon is presently under police inventory at the Franklin police department. At this time the four witnesses who were the bar patrons were returned to the above location where they were interviewed by the undersigned and Det. LOOMIS. All interviewed took the positions that they had been in.

Mr. Jeffery O. ████████, white male, age, 22, date of birth, 10-15-57 of ██████ South 60th Street, Franklin, phone (421█████). Informant stated that he was standing at the bar directly to the East of the male victim. Informant stated that at approximately 10:15PM on 1-12-80 the male victim had brought out from under his coat a large revolver, cal. unknown and was playing with it. Informant stated that the male victim did not say anything to him but passed the weapon over to the female victim. Informant stated that the female had stated " I don't want to fool with that thing" and had passed the weapon back to the male victim. Informant stated that he had stated that the male victim should stop playing with the weapon at which time the male had turned and had pointed it at him. Informant stated that he had then stated " Don't fool around and put that thing away" at which time the male victim had placed the weapon behind him. Informant stated that he had then walked over to a foosball game board which was located at a right angle to the Northwest corner of the bar and had began playing. Informant stated that a short time later he heard a shot and when he turned and looked, the female was sliding off her bar stool and against the jukebox and the male had the weapon in his left hand looking down at her. Informant stated that the male then looked once at the bartender and then again at the female at which time he had placed the weapon against his left temple and had pulled the trigger. Informant stated that he had heard the missile pass him and exit through the window. The informant stated that the male victim then sort of slipped sideways downward and had covered the females body with his. Informant stated that to his knowledge, the male and female had not been arguing at any time but were laughing and telling jokes. Informant had no additional information. Informant did state to the undersigned that the man who he was playing foosball with had ran out of the bar right after the shooting had taken place and he had no knowledge as to his name.

Mr. Michael M. ████████, white male, age, 22, date of birth, 10-22-57, of █████ South 44th Street, Franklin, phone (421-█████). Informant stated that he had been sitting at the East end of the bar and talking to the bartender. Informant stated that at approximately 10:30PM on 1-12-80 he had heard a loud noise which had sounded like a large firecracker going off. Informant stated that when he had looked up he did not see the female victim who had been sitting on the far barstool on the West side of the bar along the wall. Informant stated that the male victim was standing up facing to the West and he had a gun in his left hand. Informant stated that within a few seconds, the male victim placed the weapon to his left temple and had fired. Informant did not know where the bullet had gone but did notice a hole in the window right after the shot was fired. Informant stated that he had not heard the victims arguing and had not paid much

3420

OVER

(Cont.)

attention to them up to the time of the shooting. Informant did state that he had seen the male victim fooling around with a large gun. Informant had no additional information to give.

Mr. Donald [redacted], white male, age, 21, date of birth, 5-15-58, of [redacted] West Rawson Avenue, Franklin, phone (421-[redacted]). Informant stated that he had been shooting pool with the table located along the Southeast wall of the bar. Informant stated that his position was to the North side of the table. Informant stated that he had not paid any attention to what was going on at the other end of the bar and had no knowledge that the male victim was fooling around with a gun. Informant stated that at approximately 10:30PM on 1-12-80, he had just bent over the table to make a shot when he heard a very loud noise. Informant stated that he stood up and had looked to the West in the direction of where both victims were and had observed the male standing with his back to him and the female laying on the floor alongside the jukebox. Informant stated that he then observed the male victim raise a revolver to the left side of his head and fire. Informant stated that he was so shook up he did not know which way to go and he sort of froze there. Informant stated that the bartender had then called the police department. Informant stated that after the initial shock he had seen the female victim on her back with her head against the juke box and the males body over the top of her. Informant had no additional information.

Mr. Kennith D. [redacted], white male, age, 21, date of birth, 11-8-58 of [redacted] South 36th Street, Franklin, phone ([redacted]-9510). Informant stated that he had been shooting pool with his friend [redacted] and that he was standing with his back to the South wall and facing North at the time of the first shot. Informant stated that he also had not been aware of what was happening at the other end of the bar until he heard a loud noise. Informant stated as he looked West he observed the female on the floor and the male standing with his back to him facing the West wall. Informant stated that it was then that he saw the male victim raise a large weapon that he had in his left hand and place it against his left temple and fire. Informant stated that he froze at that point and did not know where the bullet had gone. Informant stated that the male victim had then fell forward over the body of the female who was laying on the floor with her head against the jukebox. Informant stated that the bartender had then called the police department. Informant stated that the bodies were removed by the ambulance from Franklin to an unknown hospital. Informant had no additional information.

From information given, it appears that this was a case of accidental shooting of the female victim by the male victim at which time the male had taken his own life.

William L. Harling WH

1/13/80, 5:10 AM.

The deceased's first cousin, Dwain [redacted], age 31, dob-12/28/1948, of [redacted], South Kinnickinnic Avenue, came to this office and after viewing the body made positive identification as that of DIANE L, [redacted].

E.Himmelreich EH

Marilyn Monroe

CORONER
COUNTY OF LOS ANGELES
CASE REPORT

Tape # [illegible] Start [illegible] End [illegible]

Case No. 81128

Taken by CRONK

Post Mortem at Family

Crypt # 33

Request of

NAME Marilyn Monroe AGE 36 Sex F Race C Date and Time of Death 8-5-62 3:40 AM

Place of Death 12305 Fifth Helena Dr. Brentwood

Pronounced Dead by Dr. Engelberg

Reported by Sgt. Clemmons Address W.L.A.

Phone 476-1890

Date 8-5-62 Time 5:25 A.M. (4:25 AM Duty Officer)

Phone at Scene

Police Investigation [ ] Yes [ ] No Police Agency

Officer Date Time A.M. P.M. Supplemental Request

REPORTED AS:
[ ] Natural
[ ] Accident
[ ] Suicide ?
[ ] Homicide
[ ] Undetermined
[ ]

Barbs. Overdose

Dec was removed from Bed - Covered with a sheet & Blanket

Residence of Deceased Same

Occupation Actress Religion

Employer Movie Studio

Soc. Sec. Number ?

Military No. ?

Vet. ?

Next of Kin Gladys Baker Address Phone

Relationship Mother Notified by NOT at A.M. P.M.

Weight 117 lbs. Height 65½ In. Hair Blonde Teeth U. Own L. Own Eyes Blue Mustache None

Tattoo or Deformity None Noted Condition of Body Discolored

Prints [X] Yes [ ] No Sent: FBI CII FBI No. L.A. No.

Personal I.D. By: Address

City Relationship Phone Initials and Date

Brought in by Dambacher - Pace 8-5-62 9:00 A.M. Date P.M. Door Sealed [X] Yes [ ] No

Property [ ] Yes [X] No P.A. Case? [X] Yes [ ] No P.A. Notified by Date Invest.

Remains Removed by [illegible] Release Received 8-6-62 Receipt # 177588

Released to Westwood Village on 8-6-62 By [illegible]

INQUEST [ ] Yes [ ] No Held on Inquest Deputy

Verdict: A - Noguchi - 8-5-62

CERTIFICATE ISSUED: Pending 8-7-62 By LKG FINAL By

REMARKS: obtained the following from Guy Hockett - Westwood Village mortuary. Dec was found at approx. 3:05 Am by Housekeeper Eunice Murray, who got up to check on dec, and she found the Bed Rm. door locked. She called Dr. Engelberg who came over immediately. The Dr. took the poker from the fire place & Broke the Bedroom window to gain admittance. Dr. pronounced death at 3:35 Am. The mortuary att. stated all doors to Residence were sealed. Dec. Mother is apparently in a san. Body is discolored and no evidence of any trauma

See above

C. Pace Deputy

[illegible] - 10-60 CLA

Marilyn Monroe

Obtained the following from Guy Hackett, Westwood Village mortuary. Decedent was found at approximately 3:05 a.m. by housekeeper, Eunice Murray, who got up to check on the decedent, and she found the bedroom door locked. She called Dr. Engleburg who came over immediately. The doctor took the poker from the fireplace and broke the bedroom window to gain admittance. Doctor pronounced death at 3:35 a.m. The mortuary attendant stated all doors to residence were sealed. Decedent's mother is apparently (not readable). Body is discolored but no evidence of any trauma.

Woman dies in vibrator accident

MILWAUKEE COUNTY MEDICAL EXAMINER

CASE NO. 1769

SUPPLEMENTARY

Name KATHLEEN A
Date Death 9-23-81

Wednesday, September 23, 1981: 10:00PM: Received a call from Dr. BERGER, of Deaconess hospital, reporting a death. The deceased is Kathleen A. white female, age, 37, date of birth, 7-7-44, married, of S64 W18550 Drive, Muskego, phone (679-). Informant stated that the deceased had originally entered West Allis Memorial Hospital on 8-27-81 and then was transported into the above hospital for additional treatment. Informant stated that the admitting diagnosis was Perforated urinary bladder with peritonitis, due to a vibrator being inserted into the urinary tract. The deceased expired this date at 8:50PM with the informant making the pronouncement. The informant stated that at this time, the cause of this death is Respiratory failure due to peritonitis and infection. The informant stated that the deceased's husband had alledgedly placed the vibrator into the deceased causing this injury. Informant stated that the Muskego Police Department had been to the hospital earlier this date to question the deceased, however, she could only nod her head in response to the questions asked. Informant stated that he did not know if this was a chargable case and if the Medical Examiner would be seeking an autopsy. A Medical Examiners hold was placed on the deceased pending additional investigation.

9-23-81: 10:15PM: Received a return call from Detective John Daley of the Muskego Police Department, in reference to additional information in this case. The deceased is listed as noted above, with the husband being , age, 40, date of birth, 5-25-41, of the same address. Informant stated that they had been called i. this date in the AM by Dr. Berger in reference to the same information as given to the undersigned. Informant stated that the doctor had stated that the vibrator had been placed into the bladder through the urinary tract thereby rupturing the bladder. Informant stated that from additional information received, the deceased had done this to herself with the same item in January of this year and was treated for a tear in the bladder by a Dr. WALSCH. Informant stated that Dr. Berger had stated that the same area was ruptured this time. Informant stated that the deceased had given the doctor information that her husband had abused her in the past and that they have had two trial seperations since their marrage in November 8, 1980. Informant stated that they had went to the residence and had questioned the deceased's husband, who had stated that he had inserted the vibrator into the deceased with her permission and this was only approximately 2 inches. Informant stated that they had recovered the vibrator which is a blunt plastic instrument that measures 12 inches in length and 1 1/2 inches in circumference and smooth. Informant stated that when he had spoke with the doctor on this, he was informed that to have this placed into the body in such a way would cause excruciating pain as the most that the opening would normally allow would be approximately 1 inch in circumference. Informant stated that the deceased's husband had denied that he had ever abused the deceased except once prior to their being married. The informant asked if this office would be conducting an autopsy and he was advised by the undersigned that Mr. Warren Hill would be contacted and that we would call him back.

9-23-81: 10:25PM: Contacted Deputy Medical Examiner Warren Hill and gave him the above information. Informant stated that since this originated in Muskego, the Waukesha County Coroner would be handling the case.

9-23-81: 10:30PM: Contacted Detective Daley and advised him of the above.

9-23-81: 10:30PM Contacted Mr. Donald Eggums, Waukesha County Coroner and gave him the above information. He will contact all parties involved and bring the deceased in for autopsy.

William L. Harling wlh

3420

Teen's baby found stuffed in garbage

MILWAUKEE COUNTY MEDICAL EXAMINER

CASE NO. 2036

SUPPLEMENTARY

Name BOY BABY [redacted]
Date Death 11/9/80

Sunday, 11/9/80, 7:35pm, Lt. Beasley, Milwaukee Police Detective Bureau, called and reported that officers from his department were at [redacted] West Potomac where the body of an obviously dead infant had been found. He requested an investigator respond to the scene.

The undersigned drove to the location and found it to be a two story frame single family dwelling. At the scene the undersigned was admitted to the residence by Mrs. Shirley [redacted], 8/29/26, the owner of the home. Present were Det. Radovich, Squad 205, and Det. Rose, Squad 213. They directed the undersigned to an upstairs bedroom. There the undersigned entered a walk-in closet and observed a plastic waste basket, 10" in diameter and 12" in height, on the floor. It was upright and contained folded newspapers which were partially blood soaked and one sanitary napkin which was throughly blood soaked.

The officers stated that one Patty Ann [redacted], W/F, age 19, born 10/10/61, resides at the residence with her mother, the forementioned Shirley [redacted]. The police department received a call this date from District Attorney E.Michael McCann who stated he had been contacted by a Dr. John Brennan, St. Joseph's Hospital, a personal friend of his. The physician stated he had a patient who had presented herself for treatment and who had obviously recently delivered a child. The patient denied she had had a child and the physician felt this was very possibly a criminal matter. The police were so informed and went to St. Joseph's Hospital. There they attempted to talk with the mother. She stated that on advice of her attorney she was not going to comment. The attorney is one Marvin Resnick.

The officers then interviewed the mother who also did not wish to speak with the officers about the matter. They asked her to confer with her attorney and call them back.

Atty. Resnick then called the police and stated that he had information for them that had been authorized for release to the police by the family. He stated that Patty Ann [redacted] had delivered a child at home and had wrapped the child in newspapers. She then stuffed the baby into a plastic garbage pail and put the pail in her closet. He stated that the mother was willing to take them to the residence and permit them to remove the baby from the residence.

The officers then returned to the hospital, picked-up the subject Shirley [redacted], and took her to her home. They found the plastic garbage pail as noted above and notified this office.

The undersigned asked that Ptm. Butler take several photos of the pail and that the contents be examined at the medical examiner's office; not at the scene. This was done.

Prior to leaving the residence the undersigned spoke with Shirley [redacted]. She stated that she had confered with her attorney but did not mind answering a few questions. She stated that she lived at the residence with her daughter Patty Ann. Her daughter had attended MATC, the data processing program, for one year following graduation from high school. This is a two year program. In June 1980 her daughter finished the first year but did not return this fall for the second year of the program. Patty Ann worked at a local McDonald's resturant part-time and had done so since she was 16 years old. The mother stated that she never at any time had any idea her daughter was pregnant. Last evening Patty Ann participated in her regular bowling league and the informant watched. Patty Ann bowled from 7pm to 9pm. The mother then left and her daughter remained with friends. The mother returned home at 1:00am this date to find Patty Ann laying on the livingroom couch. Patty complained of stomach cramps. She was wearing a sanitary napkin and the mother checked this finding a small amount of blood present; she felt her daughter was having her period. The daughter then stayed in the mother's bed with her until a later time. At this point the mother stated she would make no further comment. She stated that on advice of her attorney she would make no further comment on what had transpired.

The undersigned then returned to the upstairs room, took photos of the area (two black&white), and removed the plastic

3420

(continued)

garbage pail with contents to the medical examiner's squad. The ~~the~~ undersigned request Det. Radovich rode in the ME Squad to the morgue and was present during the admitting and examination. At the morgue BofI Tech Scott Hall took photos of the body and materials found with the body.

The body was wrapped in newspapers, a placenta being attached to the infant. A signed property receipt was obtained bearing the signature of Det. Radovich.

J.R.Endrizzi

Sunday, 11/9/80, 7:35pm, Additional note should be made that at the hospital the mother presented herself and stated that she had not had a child. She was admitted to the hospital at 8:30am this date. The subject Shirley ████████ stated to the officer but not to this investigator that her daughter had suffered massive hemorrhaging at approximately 3:00am. She refused to comment on why she did not seek medical attention for her daughter at once at that time.

J.R.Endrizzi

Monday, 11/10/80, 10:15 AM: Contacted Dr John Brennan at St Joseph's Hospital who said he examined Patty Ann ████████ yesterday at the hospital. He said the patient complained of having an early menstral period and denied she had ever been pregnant. Informant noted lacerations in the vagina and the patient said she probably cause the lacerations by trying to remove clots by herself. Informant said by his examination that it was obvious the woman had delivered a child and by the degree of internal eccymosis he felt someone would had to help her during labor. The woman did not mention any other treating physician to informant.

John J. Guss

Tuesday November 18,1980 1:50PM:Milwaukee County District Attorney E. Michael McCann called this undersigned at home. Informant stated that he had contacted a pathologist who would re-autopsy the deceased Boy Baby ████████. Informant requested that the body be held until that time.

David W. Livingston

Thursday, December 4, 1980: 3:05PM: Contacted Attorney Marvin Resnick, phone (271████) in reference to burial of the deceased, male baby ████████. Informant stated that District Attorney Michael McCann has had an unknown private pathologest perform another autopsy on the deceased and as of this date, he has not received the information from this. As such, he can not have the burial as he may also wish another autopsy done by a pathologest of his own. Informant will contact this office with any additional information when known.

William L. Harling

Wednesday January 14,81 11:30AM The undersigned spoke with Attny. Resnick regarding the burial of Male Infant ████████. The informant stated that he was awaiting a report from the DA's Office regarding the second autopsy on the subject. Mr. Resnick was informed that the remains were a health hazard and would be dispose of if no arrangements were made. The informant stated that he would contact the DA's office again and return a call to this office.

R. Goeb

MILWAUKEE COUNTY MEDICAL EXAMINER

CASE NO. 288

SUPPLEMENTARY

Name LULA PEARL [redacted]
Date Death 2/8/82

8:55 PM - Monday - February 8, 1982 - Detective Captain FRANKLIN called this office and said the body of a gun-shot victim awaited the services of this office at [redacted] W. McKinley.

J.Kortsch JK

Monday, 2/8/82, 9:20PM, Dr. Harlan Stueven called from County General Hospital to report that Med 7 conveyed LULA PEARL [redacted] age 48 from [redacted] West Mc Kinley. The deceased was admitted in Emergency at 8:49pm, pulseless and non-breathing in bradycardia. CPR efforts obtained no responses and death pronouncement was made at 9:05PM. The body is nude, warm and limp, blood from mouth with exposed brain matter. Informant requested to place hold on body.

C. Borchardt JK

9:15 PM - Monday - February 8, 1982 - The undersigned went to the scene and met there with Lt. WERRA, Squad #152, Detectives LORENZ and PETZOLD, Squad #109, PO CZAJKOWSKI and NIEVES, Squad #12, and PO WELLS and DOBRASKA, Squad #17.
The residence is one of the many units in the Highland Park Housing Project.
The officers at the scene cautioned the undersigned not to divulge his identity to the family members present because they were not aware that the mother of the family was dead.
The officers said the decedent is LULA PEARL [redacted], born 2-17-33, married to LEROY, 2-23-33.
The couple lived at this address with their children, GLRIA, age 18, ROSIE, age 17, CURTIS, 22, and FREDERICK, 24.
The husband was seated in a bedroom adjacent to the kitchen this Pm watching TV shows.
Deceased was seated in the kitchen at the table with her chair against the north wall.
Son FREDERICK entered the hallway between the kitchen and the living room.
The husband LEROY heard FREDERICK call out to the decedent, "Stick 'em up".
He turned away from the TV set and glanced into the kitchen.
He saw FREDERICK holding a revolver and pointing it at the deceased.
Decedent said: "Boy, you better get away from here and stop playing with that gun".
Then the gun was fired with the bullet striking deceased in the head.
FREDERICK called out: "Lord, I'm sorry, Momma, I didn't mean to do that".
He then ran from the residence still holding the gun.
The gun is a .22 calibre revolver owned by FREDERICK.
A Paramed unit removed deceased to a hospital for a death pronouncement.
The officers showed the undersigned to the kitchen with the only remarkable thing visible was a large pool of liquid blood on the floor.
The officers are of the opinion that the deceased was struck by a bullet from the gun held by her son FREDERICK but that he did not intend to harm her and the gun fired accidentally.

J.Kortsch JK

MILWAUKEE COUNTY MEDICAL EXAMINER

CASE NO. 157

SUPPLEMENTARY #1

Name JOHN WERNER JIMMI [redacted]

Date Death 1/17/81

Saturday, 1/17/81, 5:20PM, PO John Rodriquez of squad 21, called to report that he and his partner, PO James Karney, were standing by at [redacted] South 3rd Street, apartment 212 where a white male has been dead for about one week by possible electrocution. Medical Examiner requested.

Investigator James Endrizzi proceeded to scene.

C. Borchardt

Saturday, 1/17/81, 5:30pm, The undersigned arrived at the residence, [redacted] South 3rd Street, and found it to be a newer two story brick apartment building. The apartment in question, #212, is located on the second floor.

At that location the undersigned was met by Ptm. Carney and Rodriquez, Squad 21 early, Det. Apps, Squad 106 early, and other officers and neighbors. They directed the undersigned to the apartment which when entered was found to be in a neat and tidy state of array.

The body of the deceased, later identified by ID in the room as JOHN WERNER JIMMI [redacted], white male, 26 years of age, born 4/23/56, of the stated apartment, is seen laying on it's left side, knees pulled about half way up, clad in a bathrobe and slippers, obviously dead. The head is to the north and the feet to the south. The body is in an advanced state of decomposition with much purge. The body has a plastic sheet, clear plastic, positioned under the knees and lower extremities Purge is seen pooled on top of the sheet and appears to have been placed there antemortum. An electrical extention cord is seen positioned north of the body, extending from a plugged in position in the west wall, north of the body, then east of the body and then appearing to be connected to both arms at the elbows. As the circuit appears live the body had not been touched by the firemen who had been present or the police officers who had been called to the scene. The undersigned, after taking several photos of the scene, used a broom to unplug the extention cord from the wall. It was then seen that the extension cord was actually two extension cords; one plugged into the wall and a second plugged into the first, the second having it's female end cut off and the wire ends bared.

On the bed north of the body is seen an ash tray, five cigarettes laying open on the bed, and a handkerchief. There is a partial can of Pabst beer standing upright on the floor northeast of the body at the foot of the hide-a-bed couch which is open and covered with bed covers. A TV set is on and operating at the foot of the bed facing the decedent.

The position of all the items mentioned appears to yield the following most likely series of events. The deceased positioned the plastic sheeting under himself and arranged the cigarettes so that he could reach them. He then plugged in the first extension cord, that being the one being plugged into the wall outlet. He had the TV positioned so that he could watch it while he was seated on the floor. The second extension cord was fastened about his arms at the elbows; one end of each lead going to each arm. The wire ends were bared to provide good contact with the skin. The wires were fastened back on themselves so they would not fall off and it was then while seated on the floor that the decedent plugged the second cord which was fastened to his arms into the first which was already inserted into the outlet; thus completing the circuit. The body was too far away from the wall outlet to provide the decedent with the opportunity to hook the entire circuit up and then plug into the wall outlet.

In a waist basket in the kitchen a plastic TYME bank card was found cut to pieces.

On a book shelf just east of the body and laying on several books was a note. It is partially covered with men's clothing.

(continued)

3420

This is the first note found. A sealed, stamped letter was found laying on the books near the first note and it was opened to reveal it's contents. This note also indicates intent to take his own life as did the first. A receipt was found in this envelope which is the receipt the decedent received when he mailed a package to the addressee of the letter. These notes will be detailed below.

A through search of the entire apartment was conducted by the undersigned in the presence of the forementioned officers. No indication of any kind was found as to next-of-kin, medical, or mental treatment. The bathroom revealed no prescription medication and no nonprescription medication. It contained toiletries consistant with a man living alone.

The refrierator contained bread, beer, and little else. A drivers license was found with the decedent's name and date of birth and later a certificate of birth registration was found with the complete name as listed on the face sheet of this report.

The undersigned spoke with the manager of the building, Estaban [redacted], 6/13/58, Apt. 102, and his girlfriend, Renee [redacted], 8/6/56, same address, who stated that they had seen the deceased last on Monday, 1/12/81. They had a passing conversation; ie HI how are you, that type of meeting. [redacted] stated that about 3 weeks ago she encountered the deceased in a neighborhood bar where the deceased was drinking at the time. He was intoxicated at the time and stated that he was very depressed, that he was fearful of loosing his job, and that things in general were rotten. He had girlfriend troubles and couldn't get any rest. She stated she had no further discussion with him as he appeared; "Really down". Later the uniform officers, in canvasing the neighborhood encountered one Richard L. [redacted], 2/27/28, of [redacted] South 3rd Street, #207, who stated that he had seen the deceased last on the morning of 1/14/81 or 1/15/81. He could not recall which date. It was in the morning hours and the deceased had been carrying out a large box of garbage. He greeted the deceased, which greeting was returned. They did not speek further.

The officers stated that this date they had been called to the residence to investigate a possible DOA. The manager of the buildin had come to the apartment this date to collect the rent which was overdue; a very unusual situation for the decednet. He knocked and then tried the door. He found it closed but unlocked. The manager then attempted to enter and found the night chain in place. He then noted a foul stench eminating from the room. He called for the firemen who arrived and forced the door open. On finding the dedeased they caled for the polcie and left.

Among the papers found at the scene were papers indicating that the deceased had served in the US Army in Germany. Another paper indicates that on 2/2/77, the Witkowiak funeral home buried one Stanley [redacted]. born 7/23/23; possible father of the deceasedd A call to the funeral home reveals an address for Mrs. Stanley [redacted] of 911 South 4th Street, phone [redacted]-1752. A call to that number went unanswered.

As regards the first note it reads;"As A Last Request Please No Mention of this in the Media A Paupers Burial (signed) John [redacted]..Can There Possibly Be A Just God? Or Are We Just Pieces of Meat"..end of note.

As regards the second note/letter which was found inside the envelope. It is addressed to Irene Lage (or possibly Loge), 2306 Ulisch/Schonberg, West Germany. It reads in part;" Dear Irene, This is a very hard letter to write. But by doing so, I'm hoping to east the grief and anger you may feel. It's no longer possible for me to continue living in this world. I wish there was some way I could do this without bringing you any pain, perhaps if you keep the thought that I'll finally be at peace with myself..... All I truly want is a paupers burial. Would you please inform Linda of this..." He also indicates that he has mailed a package of his most valued possession. The post office insured mail receipt is included in the letter and is dated January 5, 1981.

The body was removed from the scene by the medical examiner's ambulance. Items listed were removed, a signed property receipt being obtained by the undersigned. No address book or other information about how to contact next-of-kin was found. Doors to the ambulanee locked at the scene by the undersigned. The apartment was locked and the manager instructed to admit no one.

J.R.Endrizzi

See Supp #2

MILWAUKEE COUNTY MEDICAL EXAMINER

CASE NO. 157

SUPPLEMENTARY

Name JOHN WERNER JIMMI ████

Date Death January 17, 1981

10:40 PM - Saturday - January 17, 1981 - Detective APPS called this office and said he had notified deceased's step-mother, LITIJA ████, of the death.
She said deceased was "not right in the head", unemployable, and lacked normal intelligence. She knew of no tendencies toward suicide.
She last saw him in September, 1979. She knew nothing of his medical or mental problems at this time.

J.Kortsch

Sunday. 1/18/81, 11:10am, Mrs. Litija ████, 911 South ████ Street, 643-████, called and requested additional information about this case. She identified herself as the step-mother of the deceased, JOHN ████.

She stated that the deceased's parents had seperated when he was 12 years of age. The mother took her son and daughter to West Germany with her. The father was an alcoholic. The father complained bitterly that his son had been taken from him and demanded the son's return. The mother complied and the son was returned to this county. The mother and daughter continued to live in West Germany. It was shortly after that that the mother was run over by a taxi and killed.

The decedent was very upset and having to return to live with his father, the loss of his mother, and loss of companionship with his sister, whom he loved and was very close to. The informant stated that the deceased was never the same after these events.

He had been in the US Army and had served in West Germany. On returning to Milwaukee approximately 5½ years ago, the deceased had difficulty keeping a job. He refused to get up for work, would not attend school, and had difficulty regulating himself; was not self-motivated. The informant stated she was in the process of making notification to the decedent's sister, Irene ████.

J.R.Endrizzi

3420

Man fatally stabbed in tiff over dog

MILWAUKEE COUNTY MEDICAL EXAMINER

CASE NO. 220

SUPPLEMENTARY

Name RICHARD ████

Date Death 1/24/81

Saturday, 1/24/81, 10:20PM, Dr. Grant called from County Hospital to report the death of RICHARD ████ 29, dob 9-21-1951, at 9:50PM. The deceased was conveyed by Med 6 from the 2900 block of West North Avenue and was admitted at 9:38pm with multiple stab wounds to the chest. The deceased's chest was opened but there were no responses. he body was warm and limp and clad only in trousers. Informant requested to place hold on body.

C. Borchardt CB

Saturday, January 24, 1981, 10:45PM: The undersigned and David Livingston, Assistant Deputy Medical Examiner went to 2933 North Ave., where the Top Hat of Disco Bar is located.
Upon arrival the undersigned was met by Lt. Becker, and Police Officer Pile and Hanneman, squad#104, of the Milwaukee Police Department.
Informant stated that the deceased was in the rear of the building at the south end of the bar, when an arguement over a dog started with two other partons of the bar, and the deceased started arguing with one of the people already involved in the arguement, and at that point the deceased was cut and/or stabbed by his assailant, who fled the building. The deceased was helped to the disco area of the bar, which is located near the front or north end of the bar. The deceased collapsed at that point. An outline of the deceased's body shows that the deceased was lying on the floor with his head facing north and his feet facing south. The center of the outline exhibited severa areas of blood, (liquid). There is a large area of blood at the end of the bar in the south end of the building, and a trail of blood leading to the outlined area.
Informant stated that the deceased was RICHARD ████, 29 years, dob 9-21-51, residence ████ N. 34th Street or residence ████ N. 6th Street, who is married. Informant stated that the correct address of the deceased has not yet been determined. Informant stated that the deceased is married to Sherita, residence ████ N. 34th Street, phone 442-████.
Informant stated that the deceased was in the bar with his girlfriend. Informant stated that the last name of the deceased was taken from his driver's license.

John L. O. Jones JLOJ

Sunday January 25,1981; 1:55AM

Identification Technician RICHARD FUHRMAN, Milwaukee Police Department Bureau of Identification, came to the County Morgue and took three color photos of the deceased. He also took a right index fingerprint and stated that it matched one on file for RICHARD BERNARD ████, DOB 9/21/1951, a.k.a. Richard ████, a.k.a. "Butch".

Thomas F. Hanratty TFH.

Sunday January 25,1981;5:30AM

SHERITA ████, DOB 9/16/1955, of ████ North 34th Street (442████), came to the County Morgue with Detective Terry Datka and made positive visual identification of the deceased as her husband RICHARD ████ or RICHARD ████; he used the names interchangably. The deceased lived at the same address.

Thomas F. Hanratty TFH

3420

Sharon Tate

8793
8794
8795

COUNTY OF LOS ANGELES
OFFICE OF CHIEF MEDICAL EXAMINER—CORONER
MEDICAL REPORT

Name Sharon Tate Polanski Case No. 69 8796

Date 8-9-69 Dr.

CONTINUATION SHEET

apparently entertaining a mixed group of 4 young people at [illegible] her luxurious, avant garde, ranch-estate type home. The party was noticed by neighbors down the street and nearby during that afternoon into early evening 8-8-69.

At about 12³⁰ am 8-9-69 a nearby neighbor reported later he heard a sound of shot echo about [illegible]. Approximately 9⁰⁰ AM 8-9-69 household maid reported for duty to find a scene of apparent carnage. House doors opened, some lights left on, windows ajar. An inscription in blood upon front door. One apparently dead body seated in driver's seat of late model Rambler Ambassador parked in parking area at entrance gate (John Doe 85) 69-8792.

Another apparently dead body (69-8793) crumpled to lawn in front of veranda. Body dressed casually for occasion (A/S). The third apparently dead body on lawn about 60 feet south of (69-8793) lying on back and dressed apparently for sleep. This labeled case # 69-8794. (A/S)

Two bodies - a man (69-8795) and [illegible] woman decedent were found in living room [illegible] in front of cold fire place at foot of large [illegible]. Bodies on floor. Man in casual party dress [illegible] decedent in bra and briefs. (A/S) A long [illegible] [illegible]ibly 1/4 inc. nylon cord was looped about each of [illegible] persons necks and also looped over a suppo[illegible] beam of sleeping loft over head. A bath towe[illegible] apparently placed over head of man prior to loo[illegible] of rope about neck.

A caretaker - occupying small house [illegible] end of huge lot and somewhat away from [illegible] house had entertained a young man earlier in [illegible] to about 12¹⁵ a.m. 8-9-69 when this you[illegible] [illegible] man took leave. The John Doe 85 in auto may [illegible] [illegible]ibly have been the same young man. The caretak[illegible] being questioned by police appeared unaware of a[illegible] [illegible]tation about the premises at time happened. [illegible]

— Continued —

76M110U-4-67

COUNTY OF LOS ANGELES

OFFICE OF CHIEF MEDICAL EXAMINER—CORONER

MEDICAL REPORT

Name: Sharon Tate Polanski   Case No. 69-8796

Date: 8-9-69   Dr. ____

CONTINUATION SHEET

Signs of struggle appeared localized in center of living room where decedent and 69-8795 lay upon blood soaked carpeting and amid broken bric-a-brac. Blood on flagstone on front porch covering an area of about 2'x2' and dried. Small amount blood in open garage at parking lot as also a small amount in possible foot smear upon back steps leading to swimming pool at rear of house and adjacent to body (69-8794)

No weapons nor suspects in custody. Central homicide witnessing autopsy.

Frikin

OBTAIN BLOOD AT AUTOPSY.

JG

76M118U-6-67

Sharon Tate

Apparently entertaining a mixed group of 4 young people at-in her luxurious, avant garde (not readable) estate-type home. The party was noticed by neighbors down the street and nearby during most afternoon into early evening, 8-8-69.

At about 12:30 a.m., 8-9-69, a nearby neighbor reported later he heard a sound of shot echo above hills. Approximately 9:10 a.m., 8-9-69, household maid reported for duty to find a scene of apparent carnage. House doors opened and some lights yet on and windows ajar. An inscription in blood upon front door. One apparently dead body seated in driver's seat of late model Rambler Ambassador parked in parking area at entrance gate.

Another apparently dead body crumpled to lawn in front of veranda. Body dressed casually for occasion. The third apparently dead body on lawn about 60 feet south of (other body) laying on back and dressed apparently for sleep. This labled case No. 69-8794.

Two bodies, a man and woman decedent, were found in living room in front of cold fireplace at foot of large sofa. Bodies on floor. Man in casual party dress and decedent in bra and briefs. A long possibly ¾ inch nylon cord was looped about each of these persons' necks and also looped about over a supporting beam of sleeping loft over head. A bath towel apparently placed over head of man prior to looping of rope about neck.

A caretaker occupying small house at end of huge lot and somewhat away from house had entertained a young man earlier in evening to about 12:15 a,m. 8-9-69 when this young man took leave. The John Doe in auto may possibly have been the same young man. The caretaker being questioned by police appeared unaware of apparent action about the premises at time happened.

Signs of struggle appeared localized in center of living room where decedent (Tate) and other body lay upon blood-soaked carpeting and amid broken bric-a-brac. Blood on flagstone on front porch covering an area of about 2' x 2' and dried. Small amount of blood in open garage at parking lot as also a small amount on possible foot smear upon back steps leading to swimming pool at rear of house and adjacent to body.

No weapons nor suspects in custody. Central homicide witnessing autopsy.

Man drinks poison to join bride-to-be in death

MILWAUKEE COUNTY MEDICAL EXAMINER

CASE NO. 1718

SUPPLEMENTARY

Name RICHARD ██████
Date Death September 18, 1980

Thursday, September 18, 1980, 4:20 a.m.: Received a call from Dr. Reed, Milwaukee County General Hospital, reporting a death. Deceased is Richard ██████, white male, age 20, DOB 12/2/59, single. Deceased resides at 8834 W. ██████, phone 46██████. Informant stated that the deceased was transported into the hospital from his residence dressed in underclothes, warm and limp, by Paramed Unit #4. Informant stated that he made the dead on arrival pronouncement at 3:55 a.m this date. Informant stated that the deceased has a history of attempted suicides dating back to 9/1/80. Informant stated that, from information received, the deceased had been despondent since the death of his girlfriend just prior to 9/1/80. Informant stated that when the deceased had called in on the hot line, he had indicated he intended to take his life by Potassium Cyanide. Informant stated that they had received a call on the hot line of the hospital at 2:30 a.m. from the deceased stating that he had intended to take his life. Informant stated that at that time the police department had responded to the residence. Informant stated that there was a lot of secretion in the deceased's airway and he appeared cyanotic around the face. Informant stated that the deceased was being seen by Dr. Miller, a resident psychologist at Milwaukee County General, for his prior attempts. Informant stated that it is unknown if the deceased is on any type of medications.

9/18/80, 4:35 a.m.: Contacted Detective Captain Detective Bachmann to determine if any unit had responded to the scene in reference to the above residence Informant stated that there was none as the residence was not known by the department; however, he was responding detective squad 104 at this time.

9/18/80 6:05 a.m.: Arrived at 8834 W.██████ which is a ranch-type residence located on the north side of the street. At the residence the undersigned met with Detective Robert Buska of Squad 104. Detective Buska escorted the undersigned into the residence basement area located in the northwest corner. It was observed that this area has been made up into a bedroom area. It was observed on the southeast corner of this room there is a large waterbed. Informant Buska advised that the deceased had been found in a prone position with his head to the south and feet to the north on the above bed. Informant stated that the parameds had worked on the deceased for a period of time prior to transporting the deceased to Milwaukee County General Hospital. Informant stated that from information received from the Deceased's father, Wayne H. ██████, age 55, DOB 1/11/25, same address, that the deceased had attempted to take his life four previous times to this incident. Informant stated that on the last incident the deceased had swallowed carpet cleaner, and was subsequently taken out to County General where his stomach had been pumped and treatment was made Informant stated that the deceased's girlfriend, Linda Berg, had expired from a brain aneurysm on Labor Day, and the deceased, since that time, has had no desire to live. A search of the entire area and residence showed no medications nor suicide notes from the deceased. A continued inspection of the area indicated the portion of the basement in the far southeast corner was a laundry room where there was a container of flake-type Purex all purpose bleach, some color bleach crystals, and a bottle of liquid Clorox bleach. There was also a vial indicating approximately ¼ bottle of an unknown liquid with the outside of the bottle being marked Ambesol. The undersigned also discovered an EKG strip, that had been run by the Paramed unit, along side the deceased's bed. All of the above items were taken by the undersigned and a receipt is on file with this report.

9/18/80 - 6:40 a.m.: Interviewed Mr. Wayne H. ██████, father of the deceased, and Mary ██████, age 55, mother of the deceased, in reference to any additional information in reference to this death. Informant's father stated that he had last seen the deceased at 8:30 p.m. on September 17, 1980, at which time he was leaving the residence to go out with a group of unknown friends. Deceased's mother, Mary, stated that she had awakened when her son arrived at home and had asked him what time it was, at which time he had stated, "1:00 a.m." Informant stated that she did not know if this information was correct as there was no clock in the area that she could verify this. Informant stated that she had asked the deceased if he had a good time, and the deceased had stated, "Yes." Informant stated that she had then returned back to bed and fell back to sleep. Informant stated that they had no

3420

knowledge of what the deceased had done until they were awakened by the police officer arriving at their residence at approximately 2:45 a.m. this date. Informant stated that the deceased was unemployed and had often stated that everything he did seemed to turn out wrong. Informant could give no additional information.

9/18/80, 7:00 a.m.: Contacted Investigator Dubinski at the Medical Examiner's office and requested that he check with Deputy Medical Examiner, Warren Hill, to determine if the body of the deceased should be transported into the County Morgue for autopsy. Investigator Dubinski recontacted the undersigned and stated that Deputy Medical Examiner, Warren Hill, had been contacted at 7:15 and given the above information, at which time he had stated that the deceased should be brought in. The Medical Examiner's Ambulance was dispatched at 7:15 a.m. this date. It is noted here that the undersigned received signed autopsy authorization from the deceased's mother and father and is on receipt with this file. The undersigned returned to the Medical Examiner's office.

It is also noted that on a dresser in the deceased's bedroom was found a medical dictionary that was opened to the part relating to poisons.

William L. Harling (ck) WLH

Thursday, 9/18/80, 2:15 PM: Milwaukee Police Officer Tyson, Squad 75, came to this office and turned over one bottle labeled Potassium Cyanide and one yellow pill with words "Sine-Off" written on it. The items were receipted for. The officer said deceased RICHARD ████'s father and a James E. Prellwitz, address not obtained, gave the items to him. They found the items at 1:00 AM, this date and called the police department. The items were found in a cabinet in the south room of the basement of the deceased's residence.

John J. Guss JJG

Thursday, September 18, 1980, 1:30PM: Lorraine Schmid from Milwaukee County General Hospital called this office, and stated that it would require a subpoena in order to procure the medical records of the deceased, Richard ████.

John L. O. Jones JLOJ

Boy hangs self after watching Freddie Prinze movie

MILWAUKEE COUNTY MEDICAL EXAMINER

CASE NO. 1 3 0 9 ......

SUPPLEMENTARY NO. 1

PAGE 1

Name RICHARD [redacted]
Date Death THURSDAY, JUNE 23, 1977

THURSDAY, JUNE 23, 1977, 10:10 P.M.
Police Officer G. Schneider, Squad 82 Milwaukee Police Department, called to report the death of RICHARD [redacted], 13 years old, date of birth 8-22-1963, of 920 East [redacted] Place. The subject was conveyed to Johnston Municipal Hospital where he was pronounced dead. The hospital will be instructed to call this office with details. The subject was found hanging at his home.

Thomas F. Hanratty, Medical Examiner Field Investigator in Charge dispatched.

THOMAS F. HANRATTY (sas)

THURSDAY, JUNE 23, 1977, 10:20 P.M.
Dr. Anthony Jurisic called from Johnston Municipal Hospital to report that he pronounced RICHARD [redacted], age 13, 8-22-1963, dead on arrival at 10:00 P.M. Deceased was conveyed by Squad 82 from 920 East [redacted] Street. Deceased is fully dressed, the body is warm and limp, and there is a deep groove about his neck. Informant requested to place hold on body.

C. G. BORCHARDT (sas)

Thursday June 23, 1977; 10:35PM

Arrived at 920 [redacted] Place and was met by Lieutenant R. BRANDT, Detectives A. MILLER and D. MALOCK, Squad # 106, and several uniformed police officers. Was shown to the basement of the single family residence. Near the center of the basement floor is a white chalk outline of a body, head to the East, feet to the West. Spoke to WALTER A. [redacted], 49 years old, DOB 3/26/1928, the father of the deceased RICHARD [redacted], 13 years old, above. The father, a third shift employee of Louis Allis Company, stated that he was outside this evening from about 8:00PM onward. He was recharging a auto battery, using a neighbor's recharger. At about 9:15PM, he came into the basement to put his tools away. Suddenly, he noted the body of his son, Richard [redacted], hanging from a cloth noose that was tied about a cross bar , which in turn was nailed to the rafters. The informant doesn't know for sure if the subject's feet were touching the floor or not, but the body appeared to be suspended. The father grabbed the boy's body and held it up to release the pressure about the neck. Mr. [redacted] attempted to loosen the cloth while calling for help. His other son, FRED [redacted] 19 years old, DOB 5/27/1958, and his wife, MILDRED [redacted], 44 years old, DOB 9/26/1933, came into the basement. Fred knocked down the crossbeam and the two men laid the still form onto the floor. A small knife was then obtained from the kitchen and the noose cut. The Rescue Squad arrived within minutes.

Walter [redacted], the father, told me that the deceased was not a depressed person and has never seen a doctor for any reason since infancy. He has never threatened suicide nor made any prior attempts to take his life. He was not on drugs and had no school or girl problems. The deceased's brother, Fred, confirmed this view of the subject. However, the deceased did have a temper and occasionally fought with friends.

Spoke with MILDRED [redacted], the mother of the deceased, and she revealed that the deceased had a problem over the past

OVER

weekend with his best friend. The friend pushed over a motorcycle belonging to the friend's brother and Richard told the brother who did it. Since that time, the friend would call the deceased names, i.e. "squealer", "fag", when the subject went outside. Other neighborhood children picked up on it and occasionally joined in the derision, so the past week has been uncomfortable for Richard. Tonight, the deceased and Fred had a small argument while cleaning the kitchen, but nothing of a significant nature. At about 8:00PM, Fred went outside to play "Frisbee" with neighborhood youngsters, while the mother and the deceased sat down to watch a Freddie Prinze movie on television. During the movie, the deceased got up and left the room. The mother thought that the deceased went outside until she heard her husband calling for her to call the Rescue Squad.

Examination of the area in the basement where the body was found shows that the crossbeam from which the cloth noose was hanging is 6'3" from the floor. A kitchen type chair is about one foot to the East of the area where the noose was suspended. The noose is tied around the crossbeam, then fashioned into a slipknot. The length of the cloth, with the nooses tied, is about 15". The yellow cloth was in a pile of clothing in the basement prior to the incident, and is now on file in this office. The deceased sleeps in a room with two brothers and has no place for private papers. No notes were found.

Thomas F. Hanratty

Teen slays parents; puts bodies in graves

MILWAUKEE COUNTY MEDICAL EXAMINER

CASE NO. 672 673

SUPPLEMENTARY

Name LUCILLE [redacted]

Date Death March 27, 1968

3/27/68 3:35 PM. DEPUTY INSPECTOR OF DETECTIVES KENNETH MARPLE phoned and said that a "couple" of bodies had been found at the dead end of W. Florist Avenue, which is west and north from Green Bay Avenue. Circumstances are unknown at the present time. He requests that the Medical Examiner arrange for removal of the bodies from the scene.

Medical Examiner's Ambulance dispatched at 3:38 PM. Field Investigators WARREN B. HILL & DAVID W. LIVINGSTON dispatched at 3:40 PM.

Ray. G. Gutowski

3/27/68, 4:15 PM, The undersigned along with David Livingston, also of the Medical Examiner's Office, arrived at the intersection of North Green Bay Road and West Florist Avenue. We were met by a detective who directed us west on Florist Avenue to the area of the Glendale City dump. Other police officers were present at the area where two young men claimed they had buried the bodies of their parents. In-charge at the scene were Deputy Inspector Marple, Detective Sgt. Gilbert, and Detective Sgt. Willis. The alleged burial area was pointed out to the undersigned. The area is situted about 25 feet north of a dump road which extends east off of North Flint Road and which is north of West Florist. The area is located about 4oo yards south of the Chicago-Northwestern Railroad track, and is also located about 200 yards southeast of the Glendale Police Dept. gun practice range. The ground appears to be recently dug. There is a swamp area to the immediate north of the area, and an embankment to the south leading/up to the previously indicated dump road. Present were the two sons who claimed to have buried their parents. They are Patrick [redacted], age 17 DOB 10/17/50, of [redacted] North 20th Street, and John [redacted], age 20 DOB 5/5/47, also of [redacted] North 20th Street. They directed the police to the burial area which is an area of about 4' by 4' of overturned ground. Their parents are John [redacted], age 48 DOB 3/26/19, and Lucille [redacted], age 40, DOB 5/4/27, both of [redacted] North 20th Street. Patrick, age 17, told the police that he was disgruntled with his home life. He was especially dissatisfied with his mother's conduct. On Dec. 17, 1967 at about 2:00 AM, Patrick walked into his parent's bedroom and with a .22 cal. pistol equiped with a silencer shot his mother twice in the forehead. His father was sleeping on the frontroom couch at the time. The father apparently hearing the commotion walked into the bedroom, and at that time Patrick took a .357 cal. pistol from his belt and shot his father in the head. Later in the morning John, age 20, became aware of the situation. He promised to help Patrick conceal the incident. They removed the bodies to the basement near a drain opening. Three days later they took the bodies to the above indicated location in a box. The box was placed in the dump burning area. They dug a hole to about their waist.

According to the police, relatives listed the parents as missing since they were absent for such a lengthy period of time. The sons had told relatives that their parents were on a trip to California, and they were receiving mail regularly from them. The sons were brought to the police detective bureau and questioned this AM. Patrick confessed at about 12 noon to the incident, and told the police where the bodies had been buried. The sons were taken to the dump area separately, and they both separately pointed out the burial location. More detailed information is being obtained.

A Caterpillar with a front end loader was used to remove about 12 inches of dirt from the burial location. An air hammer and shovels removed another 12 inches of soil, and at 5:05 PM, this day, the right foot and thigh of a

OVER

3420

woman, and what appeared to be left foot of a man, were uncovered. The bodies were covered with plastic sheets. The first body removed was that of a white female adult, and the removal was made at about 5:40 PM. The ground surrounding the body was fro/zen, and the body was situated about 2 feet below ground level. The female was in a pugilistic position with her head to the northwest and bent downward with the face towards the south. The legs were flexed at the knees. She was positioned on her left lateral aspects. The body is froøzen, and decomposed with extensive skin slip noted. Eyes are sunken. Hair is brown. She is dressed in nylon stockings which are attached to a garter belt which is in place. She is also wearing a white slip, white, green and yellow pajama tops with yellow buttons. There is a circular-shaped wound to the left forehead immediately above the inner aspect of the left eyebrow. The second body removed is that of a white male adult who is also in a pugilistic position with his head to the southeast and legs to th northwest. His head is also bent downward, and his legs are also flexed at the knees. He is positioned on his right lateral and posterior aspects. His legs were positioned immediatedly adjecent to the legs of the female with his left foot on top of the female's right upper leg. The remaining portions of his body was several inches below the level at which the female body was found. The male is dressed in a dark green work shirt and similar trousers. He is wearing socks, and two piece underwear. He has a wrist watch on his left wrist. The male was removed from the hole at about 6:30 PM due to thefroøzen ground. Head wounds and head fractures were noted at the scene. The bodies were placed in the Medical Examiner's ambulance at the scene, and the door of the ambulance was locked by the undersigned. The ambulance door was unlocked at the County Morgue by the undersigned.

3/27/68, 7:50 PM, Lucille Patricia ██████, DOB 7/7/48, of 745 North 25th Street, and Det, Sgt. Wills, came to the County Morgue accompanied by a police stenograpgher. Lucille Patricia is the daughter of the deceaseds. She proceeded to the morgue, and positively identified the bodies as those of her parents John and Lucille ██████, ages 48 and 40, respectively.

Warren Hill

MILWAUKEE COUNTY MEDICAL EXAMINER

SUPPLEMENTARY

CONFIDENTIAL

CASE NO. 672 & 673

Name ████, Lucille & John

Date Death

THE FOLLOWING INFORMATION TAKEN FROM MILWAUKEE DETECTIVE BUREAU RECORD ON SEPTEMBER 24, 1968:

CONFIDENTIAL

John ████, male, white, of ████ A North 20th Street, age 49, DOB, 3/25/19, married, shotgun wound to head, shooting, .22 caliber pistol, 357 magnum revelver.

On Sunday, 12-17-67, at 2:00 AM, PATRICK ████ shot his mother twice in the head which she was asleep in bed in their home at ████ A North 20th Street. The father, JOHN, got out of bed and he fired twice at him with a 357 magnum revolver, striking him once in the back of the head. He then shot him twice more in the head with a .22 caliber automatic pistol. JOHN was asleep in his bedroom and was awakened by the gunshots. He saw his father on the floor and his mother and he knew they were dead. PATRICK was holding the .22 caliber pistol with silencer. He told him not to call the police. They sat around until 7:00 AM. at which time they took both bodies into the basement. JOHN states that PATRICK knew of a place to dispose of the bodies. On Friday, 12-21-67, they wrapped the bodies in plastic and put them in a box and placed them in the trunk of their fathers auto, a 1963 stud. A friend of PATRICK, JOHN, drove them to the dump in Glendale. They buried the bodies and then the next day, Saturday, they took a taxi back to the dump and finished burying them. The two guns were confiscated by the Treasury Department. Patrick's reason for shooting was that he was having trouble with his mother. PATRICK ████, white, 17 years old and JOHN ████, white 20 years old.

Detectives: Edward Mc Hugh and Donald Johnson.

Dellos Gaatz D.G.

CONFIDENTIAL

3420

Man stricken while viewing "Orgy of Pain" peep show

MILWAUKEE COUNTY MEDICAL EXAMINER

CASE NO. 1 7 5 6

SUPPLEMENTARY NO. 1

Name BLAIN V. [redacted]

Date Death WEDNESDAY, AUGUST 31, 1977

PAGE 1

WEDNESDAY, AUGUST 31, 1977, 6:30 P.M.
Police Officer Gorecki, Milwaukee Police Squad 12A, called and reported the results of the investigation conducted by he and his partner, Police Officer Hacker, into the death of the deceased, BLAIN V. [redacted], white male, 12-24-1920, of 828 North Milwaukee Street. He stated that the deceased had been in the Denmark Book Store, 626 West Wisconsin Avenue, a bookstore which specializes in sexually oriented material. A clerk, Ottis F. [redacted], white male, 12-3-1948, of [redacted] West Kaul Avenue, 358-1146, stated that the deceased was a regular customer. He stated that the deceased had been in the store several times during the day and that on each visit he would ask for several dollars worth of change, in quarters, for the operation of a peep show projector located in the rear of the store. Each of these peep show booths consists of a seat and viewing screen located within a small cubicle which has a door which locks from the inside. Mr. [redacted] stated he remembered the deceased entering the store shortly before 4:00 P.M. At that time, the deceased obtained several dollars worth of quarters and retired to the rear projection rooms. At approximately 5:25 P.M. another customer approached [redacted] and stated that there was a man in one of the back booths whom he believed to be intoxicated. Swieger then went to the deceased's booth and found the door locked. He rapped on the door several times and received no answer. In continuing his pounding, the door's lock broke and he entered finding the deceased in a seated position and in an unconscious state. The police were then summoned. The deceased had watched a film entitled "Orgy of Pain" and the film is so constructed that for each quarter deposited, a short segment of the film is shown. It is not known exactly how long the deceased had been in the booth nor how many segments of the film he had seen. The officer stated that no attempts to notify next of kin had been made and that such notification would be left to this office.

JAMES R. ENDRIZZI (sas)

WEDNESDAY, AUGUST 31, 1977, 8:45 P.M.
The undersigned drove to the Denmark Book Store, 626 West Wisconsin Avenue and there interviewed the Manager, Ottis [redacted], 12-3-1948, of [redacted] West Kaul Avenue. He stated that he had come on duty at 4:00 this evening and that prior to that time the Assistant Manager had been in charge of the store. The undersigned then interviewed Greg [redacted], white male, 10-13-1951, of [redacted] North 24 Street, the Assistant Manager. He stated that during the course of the day the deceased had been in several times, first between 11:00 and 11:30, then between 1:00 and 1:30 and then again between 3:00 and 3:30 P.M. The deceased was a regular customer and oftentimes obtained change to use the peep show projectors located in the rear of the store. This date the deceased had change with him and did not ask for change from the informants. Mr. [redacted] and Mr. [redacted] both stated that they did not know exactly when the deceased returned to the store; however Mr. [redacted] stated it must have been prior to 4:00 P.M. as he could not recall having seen the deceased enter this date. On each occasion, the deceased would not brouse through the magazines located in the front of the store but would go directly to the peep shows. Mr. [redacted] then directed and accompanied the undersigned to the rear peep show booth area. It is reached by passing through a set of swinging doors and one then encounters 12 individual booths, each booth has a partition running from floor to ceiling and is approximately 2 feet by 3 feet. A screen is mounted on the inside of the door and the doors are secured by a bolt permitting complete privacy in viewing. Mr. [redacted]

3420

(O V E R)

stated that at approximately 5:15 P.M. he had been informed by an unknown patron that there was a "drunk" in one of the booths. Mr. ██████ then went to Booth No. 6 and looked on the door. He noted that the vacant sign was lit indicating that a movie was not being shown. He received no response and found the door locked from the inside. He then forced the dead bolt but could not open the door and observed that he was unable to do so because of a body lying on the floor. He was able to push the door open sufficiently to expose the door hinges which he removed with a pair of pliers. By this time, police officers had arrived, the door was removed and the deceased was seen lying on his left side, head to the west and feet to the northeast, in a fetal position. He was unresponsive and was conveyed by the officers.

The undersigned then drove to 828 North Milwaukee Street after having first consulted with the City, Telephone, and Street Address Directories for a listing for the deceased without success. The address is a multiple family apartment building and Apartment No. 6 is listed to "██████ and ████████". The undersigned then rang the bell for that apartment and subsequently interviewed Vernon ████████, white male, 10-20-1927, 272██████. He identified himself as the deceased's roommate and stated he had known the deceased since 1958. He stated that the deceased was divorced and had a daughter, Rebecca ████, living in Tipton, Georgia, 1-912-382-█████. He also informed the undersigned of several other relatives. He stated that he had last seen the deceased when he left for work this morning and stated he later called the deceased at 10:30 A.M. by phone. The deceased is not employed and receives Social Security disability payments due to a severe heart condition. Since 8-26-77, the deceased has been continually complaining of nausea. The deceased has been under the care of Dr. A. Cartes and last saw the doctor approximately 1 and 1/2 weeks ago. Mr. ██████████ stated that the deceased took several types of medication for his heart condition.

The undersigned called the home of Hoyt ████████, Moultrie, Georgia, 1-912-985-█████, and spoke with the deceased's sister-in-law, Mildred ████████. The undersigned informed her of the death of the deceased and she stated she would make funeral arrangements.

JAMES R. ENDRIZZI (sas)

Thursday September 1,1977 11:20AM: Dr. A. Cartes returned a call from this office. Informant stated that he had known the deceased BLAIN ████████, as a patient, for many years. The deceased was a severe hypertensive and had had a myocardial infarction in the past. Informant had seenthe deceased recently andwill signthe death certificate listing the cause of death as being heart related.

David W.Livingston DWL

About the author

James Romenesko, 28, is a reporter for The Milwaukee Journal.

He has been assigned to the police beat since August 1977. Over the years, he has read more than 1500 coroner's reports as a part of his job.

Printed at The Times-Reporter
Walworth, Wisconsin